MARINER

by Don Nigro

SAMUEL FRENCH, INC.

45 WEST 25th STREET   NEW YORK 10010
7623 SUNSET BOULEVARD   HOLLYWOOD 90046
LONDON   *TORONTO*

Mariner was originally commissioned by the Ohio State University Department of Theatre, Firman H. Brown, Chairman, and was first produced on May 8, 1991 in the Thurber Theatre in Drake Union at the Ohio State University in Columbus, Ohio with the following cast:

Princess Juana the Mad	Kim Turney
Lucinda/Desdemona/3rd Native, Mermaid, Chinese	Marnie Kerby
Mama/Pig Woman/Isabella	Megan Freeman
Felipa/Maid	Angela Dillion
Nurse/Marquesa de Moya/Estrella	Nancy Wilinski
Beatriz/Crow Woman	Kim Ryan
Rosaura/Crocodile Girl/2nd Native, Mermaid, Chinese	Annette Dariano
Maria/1st Native, Mermaid, Chinese	Michelle Sprinkles
Torquemada	David Bugher
Columbus	Shane Henry
Moniz/Bobadilla/Pinzon	Agustin Nieves
Rodrigo/Headless Man/Jester	Vance Barnes
Beggar/Dr Slawkenbergius/Ferdinand	Steve Grunkemeyer
Diego/Two-Headed Man/2nd Vivaldi/Francisco	Jeff Palisin
Ancient Mariner/1st Vivaldi/Vespucci/Emperor	Jim Gaylord
Dirty Carlos/Prince John/Prosecutor	Melvin James
Director	Don Nigro
Set designer	Russell Hastings
Costume designer	Susan S.B. Brown
Lighting designer	Cynthia Stillings
Sound designer	Jim Knapp
Technical director	Mark Shanda
Stage manager	Timothy D. Allwein
Assistant to the set designer	Dennis Hassen
Assistant to the lighting designer	Paula Rojo-Vega
Assistant technical director	Brad Powers
Assistant stage manager/Understudy for Juana	Mollie Levin
Assistant stage manager	Heather Wetmore
Master electrician	Wendy Werman
Costumer	Julia Weiss
Scenic studio supervisor	Ronald Cannell
Speech and voice coach	Susan Leigh

The playwright also wishes to thank the good people at the Thurber House in Columbus, where he was James Thurber Writer in Residence in the fall of 1988 and the spring of 1991, living in the squirrel haunted attic where the bed fell, by the mulberry tree.

CHARACTERS

Torquemada
Columbus
Moniz/Bobadilla/Pinzon
Rodrigo/Headless Man/Jester
Beggar/Dr Slawkenbergius/Ferdinand
Diego/Two Headed Man/2nd Vivaldi/Francisco
Ancient Mariner/1st Vivaldi/Vespucci/Emperor of China
Dirty Carlos/Prince John/Prosecutor

Princess Juana the Mad
Lucinda/Desdemona/3rd Native/3rd Mermaid/3rd Chinese
Mama/Pig Woman/Isabella
Felipa/Maid
Nurse/Marquesa de Moya/Estrella
Beatriz/Crow Woman
Rosaura/Crocodile Girl/2nd Native/2nd Mermaid/2nd
    Chinese
Maria/1st Native/1st Mermaid/1st Chinese

SET

The wreck of the *Santa Maria*, bow UR, stern UL, with practical crow's nest on mast UC that has fallen through the deck, thus making the crow's nest much lower than it would have been ordinarily, tattered sails, the DC part of the ship broken open on the reef to form three descending groups of levels, one from C to CR to DR, with trunks and wreckage forming thronelike structure RC with disgorged Captain's bunk forming practical bed below, one from C to CL to DL with similar thronelike structure CL with dinghy stuck on reef below, and one set of descending levels of wreckage and reef to form irregular staircase structure from C to UDC, with arches between R and C and between C and L descending structures through which players may enter and exit from underneath the ship structure. Other exits from escape stairs UR, UC behind ship, UL, L and R, and exits DL and DR at stage level. Access behind structure from any escape to any other must be easy. At DL and DR on stage level two wooden round tables with wooden stools for tavern scenes, etc. No part of the set moves mechanically, no non-actors ever onstage either at intermission or between scenes—in fact there is no space between any scenes, the action of each act is fluid and continuous, each part of the set becomes whatever is happening there at any given moment. Every part of the set must be easily accessible from every other part, with as many ways to get from any spot on the set to any other as possible. The edge of the stage is the shore, the audience is in the water. The way the play moves is always a part of the play.

ACT I

1 (Inquisition)

The MUSIC plays in the darkness as LIGHTS come up slowly on the shipwreck and the people appear one by one, each drawn in some way by the water. First COLUMBUS, up on the ship, looking downstage out to sea. Then JUANA appears from DL, throwing rocks in the water, unhappy. RODRIGO climbs up into the crow's nest. The ANCIENT MARINER fishes off the dinghy. LUCINDA and MARIA play with a large ball on the shore. BEATRIZ dangles her bare legs over the side of the ship, barefoot. FELIPA is curious about the fishing and the ANCIENT MARINER demonstrates how to bait the hook and cast her line. The NURSE is looking for Felipa, and is hit on the head by the ball. MAMA scolds the girls and tries to aid the Nurse. DIEGO admires ROSAURA, who is sunning herself on the sand, her skirt pulled up and her top down low on her arms. HE sneaks up on her as SHE leans her head back and steals an upside down kiss. SHE is startled and THEY quarrel. The BEGGAR is chased away and beaten by Felipa's uncle, MONIZ, who goes up to get her away from the Ancient Mariner. BEATRIZ gives the Beggar a piece of bread and HE admires her legs. DIRTY CARLOS wanders on with bottle, brooding. DIEGO and ROSAURA make up and kiss. All this happens in a nice, easy flow with the music,

9

*overlapping in time, a tapestry of people. The feeling
should be much like what is described in the first
chapter of* Moby Dick, *of the irresistible way people are
drawn mysteriously to the water. COLUMBUS has
been making his way down the steps, relating to the
people in various ways, a friendly man, easy to like,
who flirts with and charms the women, makes the
FISHERMAN laugh at some unheard joke, plays with
the GIRLS and gives the crying JUANA a flower and
gets her to smile. HE has moved to the DC edge of the
stage as the MUSIC ends peacefully, all the PEOPLE
now looking out at the water, perhaps a ship has
appeared on the horizon, meaning something different to
each of them. Then this idyllic scene is shattered by an
enormous, terrifying THUNDERCLAP, sudden WIND
and DARKNESS, flashes of LIGHTNING in eerie
BLUE LIGHT, and COLUMBUS finds himself
disoriented in a nightmare landscape full of screaming
and running PEOPLE, is finally left isolated DC, back
to the audience, as UC on the shipwreck appears
TORQUEMADA, the Grand Inquisitor, a fierce-looking
old man who stares grimly down at him. The STORM
quiets.*

TORQUEMADA. So. You're the subject.

COLUMBUS. Where am I? What place is this?

TORQUEMADA. That is what demons say when
they've been summoned.

COLUMBUS. I'm not a demon. I'm the Admiral of the
Ocean Sea, and I demand to know who's addressing me, and
what place this is.

TORQUEMADA. This is the Grand Tribunal. I am the Chief Adjudicator. And you are the subject of this Inquisition.

COLUMBUS. But I'm not a heretic.

TORQUEMADA. Only a heretic would presume to categorize himself. That's MY job.

COLUMBUS. I know you. You're Torquemada, the Queen's confessor.

TORQUEMADA. I am God's humble instrument.

COLUMBUS. But you're dead, you died years ago.

TORQUEMADA. I try not to let it get me down.

COLUMBUS. But how can you—

TORQUEMADA. Just shut up and try to pay attention, all right? We haven't got forever. Well, I suppose theoretically we DO have forever, but I'd prefer to wrap this thing up a little sooner than that, I've got to turn up the heat on a couple of Manicheans. Now, this Inquiry is being held to determine the fate of your immortal soul.

COLUMBUS. This is a nightmare.

TORQUEMADA. No, life is a nightmare. This is death.

COLUMBUS. I was lying in my bed, I was ill, my sons were around me, and then suddenly—

TORQUEMADA. Is there anyone present moronic enough to want to say anything in behalf of this wretched sinner? No? Good. So, consequently—

JUANA. (*Who has been huddled under the covers, sticking her head out.*) I do. I want to say something.

TORQUEMADA. No you don't.

JUANA. Yes I do. You have to let me speak, it's in the rule book, look it up.

TORQUEMADA. There is no rule book. God whispers the rules in my ear as I go along.

JUANA. I demand the privilege of royalty to speak.

TORQUEMADA. There is no royalty in hell.

JUANA. Nonsense. Hell is full of royalty.

TORQUEMADA. Oh, all right, let the record show that speaking in defense of the accused is Princess Juana la Loca of Spain, daughter to Queen Isabella and King Ferdinand, and a notorious lunatic.

JUANA. Thank you. You're very kind.

COLUMBUS. Wait a minute. I object to this. I—

TORQUEMADA. One more word from you and I'll have thumb screws fastened on your testicles.

(COLUMBUS pictures that and shuts up.)

JUANA. Don't worry, Christopher. I know what I'm doing.

(SHE pulls a fish out of her bosom and gives it to the Beggar. She is a lovely girl, dressed somewhat out of order, and she speaks like a defense counsel to the court—that is, to Torquemada, the people scattered about watching on the shipwreck, and to the audience sitting in the ocean. While she is speaking, COLUMBUS will slip away upstage and disappear for a moment under the shipwreck structure.)

JUANA. I know this man. Whenever I smell the ocean, I think of my mother's mad Italian sailor. I always felt close to him—we insane people must stick together, and shared madness is what love is. Part of my own particular form of lunacy is that I can see and smell things that aren't there. Which is ridiculous, because if you can see or smell it then it must be there, whether anybody else knows it or not. A dog can hear things you can't. Just because a rock can't see you, doesn't mean you're not there. Just because a horse can't count doesn't mean that long division is any more an illusion than horse poop. My mother's mad Italian sailor was just like that. Not like horse poop, I mean he could see things that weren't there. We both had wonderfully vivid hallucinations, his being that one could go east by sailing west, which is like winning a race by running in the wrong direction, or making one's self invisible by removing one's clothing, which is exactly what I'm going to do right now, to illustrate this very important philosophical concept.

TORQUEMADA. That won't be necessary, thank you.

JUANA. Oh, that's all right, I don't mind.

TORQUEMADA. There are no naked women in hell. Just tell us please how the accused came to your attention.

JUANA. He was vomited up from the ocean, and spewed onto the shore. He was the product of a violent oceanic ejaculation, onto the shore of Portugal.

2 (Castaway)

Cry of GULLS. A coastal village in Portugal. LUCINDA, a young girl, is trying to pull her MAMA out of their

*house. There is no break here—the action from scene to
scene is continuous always.*

LUCINDA. Mama, Mama, come quick.

MAMA. I don't do anything quick.

LUCINDA. But you've got to come, there's a body
washed up on the shore, it must be one of the sailors from
the ship that sank in the storm.

MAMA. Stay away from dead bodies, Lucinda, they're
full of disease and do not make good conversation.

LUCINDA. But, Mama, when I bent down to look at
this body, it put its hand up my skirt and caressed my
buttocks.

MAMA. Oh, it did, did it? I will deal with this myself.
If this body is not presently dead, it will be soon.

*(But as SHE is turning to go, there suddenly before her is
      COLUMBUS, younger, wet, ragged, most of his
      clothing gone.)*

COLUMBUS. Excuse me.

MAMA. AHHHHHHHHH. (*SHE puts Lucinda behind
her and makes the sign of the cross at him.*)

LUCINDA. That's the dead body that caressed my
buttocks. It followed me home. Can we keep it, Mama?

MAMA. Stay back, you. I have a knife.

COLUMBUS. I hardly think a lovely lady like yourself
would be carrying a knife around with—

MAMA. (*Producing a very ugly looking knife from the
pocket of her skirt.*) I was just about to castrate the pig.
I'm very good at that.

COLUMBUS. (*Stepping back and instinctively covering himself.*) I believe you, Madam, and, if I may say so, I'm certain that any pig would go gladly under your hand. You will I hope excuse my broken Portuguese, I've learned it from sailors, and they talk a lot but not so well. Allow me to introduce myself: I am Cristoforo Colombo, from Genoa, an Italian mariner, and the Dutch ship I was sailing on sank last night in the tempest. Please, I am completely at your mercy, you may turn me in to the authorities and allow them to execute me if you wish, I will not resist, I would not do you that insult, and if I must die, perhaps it is better I should die by the hand of such a beautiful and charming woman as yourself. Please, use the knife, take my life, here, I am your servant, do with me what you will, but first allow me, if I might, to kiss your hand, as one last taste of life, and what a lovely hand it is, madam, it is an honor to kiss and to die by this white hand.

(*SHE is watches him warily as HE kisses her hand, then up her arm, but HE finds his nose touching the tip of her knife as he gets to her elbow.*)

MAMA. That is enough kissing for the present.

COLUMBUS. Forgive me, I lost my head, in the presence of such overpowering beauty I am a child once more.

LUCINDA. Oh, don't turn him in, Mama, please, it isn't his fault we're at war with the Dutch, he isn't even Dutch, he's Italian, and he's so beautiful, oh, please don't hurt him.

MAMA. This man, my dear, is full of bullshit up to his ears.

LUCINDA. Yes, but I like it, Mama. Please? You don't want them to execute him, do you?

MAMA. They won't execute him. We're not at war with the Italians.

LUCINDA. But if they knew he came off the Dutch ship, they might.

MAMA. (*Looking at Columbus, thinking about it.*) Would Mr. Beautiful Italian Bullshit like something to eat?

COLUMBUS. Madam, I could feast upon your eyes alone, for all eternity, but if you had a little cool water, and perhaps a slice of bread, butter would be nice, maybe a bit of cheese, some sausage and wine, Burgundy would be good, and if you happen to have some chicken, I love white meat, breasts are my specialty—(*This last phrase uttered as HE gazes at the lovely Lucinda.*)

MAMA. (*Pulling his head away from her daughter by the hair.*) First we'll find you something to wear. We can't have you running around like Adam, or my daughter will begin to think she's Eve, and start playing with your serpent. (*Getting clothes from the dinghy.*) Try these. My late husband died in them.

(*COLUMBUS begins putting on clothes as the BEGGAR brings out the round wooden table from DL and LUCINDA puts food on it.*)

TORQUEMADA. (*Who has been observing all this from upstage with JUANA.*) Do you consider it a part of this man's defense that he was accomplished at bullshit?

JUANA. But this was the thing, you see, that allowed him to survive—the mad Italian sailor could charm just about anyone into doing just about anything, almost, not quite, at first, but he did no harm, it was all for the greater glory of God that the words flowed out of him like water from a fountain, he was like magic, and this magic helped him achieve his necessary end, which was always Christian and noble.

3 (Sausages)

COLUMBUS begins eating as LUCINDA beams over him. The BEGGAR lurks, trying to steal food.

MAMA. Lucinda, go slop the pigs.
LUCINDA. But I want to watch him eat, Mama. He eats so beautifully.
MAMA. GO.
LUCINDA. Yes ma'am. I'll see you later, Cristoforo.

(SHE smiles significantly at Columbus. MAMA smacks her bottom and SHE goes.)

COLUMBUS. You don't trust me, do you, Mama?
MAMA. Only an idiot would trust a man like you.
COLUMBUS. You fear I will do something natural to your daughter.
MAMA. Not if you want to continue to urinate standing up, you won't.

COLUMBUS. (*Surreptitiously feeding the Beggar under the table like a dog.*) I'll tell you, Mama—ah, this is wonderful sausage, mmm—how you can get rid of me quickly and save your lovely daughter from me forever.

MAMA. I could turn you in and see if there's a reward.

COLUMBUS. But you won't because you're a good person and you like me. What you can do instead is tell me who is the richest owner of boats in this part of Portugal.

MAMA. Señor Rodriguez, of course.

COLUMBUS. And does Señor Rodriguez have any daughters? Mmmm, the bread is excellent.

MAMA. Señor Rodriguez has all sons. Why? Are you planning to deflower all the girls in Portugal one by one?

COLUMBUS. And who is the second richest owner of boats?

MAMA. Eusabio Pedrales.

COLUMBUS. Does he have daughters?

MAMA. Yes, four.

COLUMBUS. Are they married? The wine is very good.

MAMA. Three are married, one is not.

COLUMBUS. And the unmarried one, is she beautiful?

MAMA. She has a face like a horse. Out of kindness I will not say which end.

COLUMBUS. And who is the next richest owner of boats?

MAMA. That would be Señor Perestrello, except that he's dead. But there is one daughter, unmarried, sixteen, very beautiful, but she's in Lisbon, at the house of her uncle Moniz, who guards her like a wolf.

(We have been watching FELIPA and her Nurse get ready to go to church, with MONIZ by the R throne.)

COLUMBUS. A house in Lisbon, that's good, that's very good. And tell me, Mama dear, when Señor Moniz and his beautiful niece are in Lisbon, where do they go to church?

MAMA. You are a very wicked man. Why do I like you so much?

(SHE discovers the Beggar and beats him. HE takes the table away, SHE the stool.)

TORQUEMADA. So he uses the church to get what he wants, does he?

JUANA. Oh yes, he's a very religious man.

4 (Church)

Church bells and stained glass shadows across the stage. TORQUEMADA and JUANA in church with MARIA praying, the ANCIENT MARINER sleeping. FELIPA has said goodbye to Moniz and entered the church, where COLUMBUS is counterfeiting a swoon for her benefit.

COLUMBUS. Ohhhhh.

FELIPA. Nurse, I believe that man is ill.

NURSE. Don't look at him, child. A lady does not ogle men in church.

FELIPA. Then why do we come?

NURSE. Hush. Shame on you.

FELIPA. But he's ill. Is it not the Christian thing to help him? Sir, are you all right?

COLUMBUS. Yes, yes, it's nothing, please do not disturb yourself. Ohhhhhhh.

(HE swoons and SHE catches him in her arms.)

NURSE. Felipa, you mustn't touch this person. You've not been introduced. People are staring. We do not embrace the poor here, this is a church.

FELIPA. Oh, don't be stupid, Nurse, this man requires attention.

COLUMBUS. Don't put yourself out. I'm not sick, I'm merely starving to death. I'm a lost Italian sailor, and I haven't eaten for, I don't know, a week, a month, I can't remember, but don't trouble yourself, I'll just lie on the floor until I have enough strength to crawl into the alley and expire with dignity.

FELIPA. Don't be silly, we'll take care of you. Nurse, have Pepe bring the coach around. We'll take this man home and give him something to eat.

NURSE. This is impossible. I forbid it. Your uncle will murder us.

FELIPA. Nurse, what would Jesus have done?

NURSE. Yes, and look what happened to him.

FELIPA. I can handle my uncle, you just get the coach.

NURSE. But Felipa, my honey dove, my sweetie, my baby chicken—

FELIPA. I am not your baby chicken, I'm quite grown up, now do as I say, we're fulfilling our Christian duty here, nothing more, and, besides, Italian men have such beautiful eyes, don't you think?

NURSE. Your uncle will eviscerate you.

FELIPA. No, he'll forgive me. He might eviscerate YOU. Then you can have the satisfaction of knowing you were right. Now go on, go ON.

(The NURSE goes, flustered and exasperated, as FELIPA leads COLUMBUS up to the bed, where HE takes off his pants and crawls in.)

TORQUEMADA. This sort of deception in church is inexcusable.

JUANA. What deception? He was hungry, he was tired, he threw himself upon her mercy, and she caught him. He's quite innocent.

5 (Soup)

A COCK crows. Morning. COLUMBUS in Felipa's bed, sitting up. SHE sits beside him, feeding him soup which Maria has brought.

FELIPA. Feeling better this morning?

COLUMBUS. I feel much better. This is delicious.

FELIPA. You had a very peaceful night, for the most part, except for those three or four times when you cried out and I came to comfort you, and you clutched onto me so fiercely in your sleep. Poor man, were you dreaming of your shipwreck?

COLUMBUS. Yes, it was awful, I must have been imagining in my sleep that you were the piece of wood I clung to as I swam to shore. You've saved my life.

FELIPA. I hope you didn't do to that piece of wood what you did to me, or I'd be jealous and you'd have splinters in a bad place.

NURSE. (*Bursting in backwards, trying to keep Moniz out.*) No, sir, please, you can't go in, she isn't decent—

MONIZ. (*Pushing past her.*) She certainly isn't. You— what are you doing in that girl's bed?

COLUMBUS. Eating soup. It's very good. Would you like some?

MONIZ. Don't offer me soup, you lecherous scum—

FELIPA. Uncle,—

MONIZ. Silence, whore.

COLUMBUS. Sir, I assure you, this is a perfectly innocent situation. I have simply spent the night in your niece's bed, it was an act of Christian charity. What would Jesus have done?

MONIZ. Not diddled my niece, I hope. Do you take me for an idiot?

COLUMBUS. I don't know, I've just met you.

MONIZ. How DARE you invade my home, disgrace my niece, and then sit there complacently slurping soup? Prepare to die. (*HE pulls out a small sword.*)

FELIPA. Uncle, NO.

COLUMBUS. Now, just a minute. (*Getting up, HE spills soup in his lap.*) AHHHHHHH. OOOOOOO. AHHHHH.

(*MONIZ lunges, COLUMBUS leaps away, trying to cover himself with the blanket.*)

COLUMBUS. Sir, I was ill, I did very little, I promise you—
FELIPA. Let him alone, Uncle. I love him.
COLUMBUS. (*Dodging a furious lunge by MONIZ.*) Sir, is this a bad time to enquire if I might borrow a boat from you for a little voyage to China?
MONIZ. I'LL KILL HIM. AHHHHHHHHH.

(*HE is chasing COLUMBUS all over the room, with FELIPA and the NURSE trying desperately to stop them, and TORQUEMADA and JUANA diving to get out of the way. FELIPA throws herself around her uncle's neck from behind.*)

FELIPA. If you hurt him I'll kill myself.
COLUMBUS. No, don't do that. I've got to go, anyway. (*HE's struggling to get his pants on.*) I have an appointment at the madhouse.
NURSE. I'm not surprised.
COLUMBUS. Goodbye, my love. I shall return.

(*HE tries to kiss Felipa goodbye, but MONIZ is swinging the sword, so he kisses the Nurse instead.*)

COLUMBUS. Pass it on.

(*HE runs out. FELIPA collapses in tears on the bed.
MONIZ storms and fumes, the NURSE trying to calm
him.*)

TORQUEMADA. What did he want in the madhouse?
A lifetime membership?
JUANA. (*Showing him her card.*) I have one. You
should try it, you'd fit right in. It's a lovely place.

6 (Madhouse)

COLUMBUS *wanders through the madhouse as various
LUNATICS pass by.*

DESDEMONA. (*Screaming, with the hands of a large
rag doll around her throat like a necklace, holding its legs
out and tugging so that the doll appears to be strangling
her.*) AHHHHHHHHH. AAHHHHHHHHHHHHH.
COLUMBUS. (*Avoiding Desdemona, HE bumps into
the PIG WOMAN, a ragged lady carrying a stuffed pig.*) I
wonder if you could tell me where I could find the one they
call the Ancient Mariner.
PIG WOMAN. (*Pointing her pig at him.*) OINK.
OINK. OINK. OINK. OINK.
HEADLESS MAN. (*Arms outstretched, head hidden
under his coat, stumbling into Columbus.*) The crows have
eaten my head. The crows have eaten my head. (*H E*

clutches onto Columbus.) What have you done with my head?

CROW WOMAN. (*Dressed in black with a stuffed crow attached to her shoulder, chasing the Headless Man away.*) CAWWW. CAWWWW. CAWWWW. CAWWWW.

HEADLESS MAN. (*Screaming, stumbling away, running around blindly.*) AAHHHHHHH. AHHHHHHHH.

DESDEMONA. (*Running back into Columbus.*) AAHHHHHHH. AHHHHHHHH.

COLUMBUS. (*Trying to get away from these alarming people, HE comes upon a very pretty and calm-looking girl.*) Excuse me, could you tell me—

MARIA. (*Pulling her blouse up to reveal her bare stomach.*) How dare you cast your eyes upon my tummy button, sir. Do you not know that I am the Virgin Maria, Mother of God?

COLUMBUS. I beg your pardon.

MARIA. No, it's too late to beg, but I forgive you anyway. I am, as you may know, full of grace.

COLUMBUS. Thank you.

MARIA. I am also Maria Magdalena, and Maria the sister of Martha who washes your feet, and Maria the soup bringer, and Mary Queen of Scots, and Mary Quite Contrary, and Mary Old England, and Mary Christmas and a Happy New Year.

CROCODILE GIRL. (*Speaking through her crocodile hand puppet.*) Have you brought my crocodiles?

COLUMBUS. Uh, no, I forgot, actually I was looking for—

CROCODILE GIRL. I cannot breathe without my crocodiles around me.

COLUMBUS. I'll bring some with me next time I come.

CROCODILE GIRL. Bless you. You are a good man. Would you like to suck on my breasts? I have three.

COLUMBUS. That would be nice, but I wonder first if you could tell me please where I could find the one they call—

DR. SLAWKENBERGIUS. (*A wild looking man in a pointy hat, ambushing him from behind and yanking him away.*) YOU ARE THE ONE. I KNOW YOU. THOU ART THE MAN.

COLUMBUS. (*Bewildered and disoriented.*) Pardon me?

DR. SLAWKENBERGIUS You're the blockhead who wants to sail off the end of the world.

COLUMBUS. How on earth did you know that I—

DR. SLAWKENBERGIUS. The insane are not entirely unobservant. Now, let us look into this question of the shape of the world upon which we sneeze and propagate and do wooky wooky like the fuzzy little beasties—

COLUMBUS. Are you by any chance the old sailor who—

DR. SLAWKENBERGIUS. (*Holding Columbus around the neck.*) SILENCE. DO YOU WANT TO WAKE UP GOD? Now, I have here—(*Dragging Columbus over to a table brought out by a man with two heads.*)—thank you, my friends.

TWO HEADED MAN. (*Low voice.*) Thank you. (*High voice.*) You're welcome. (*Low voice.*) Not you, dung face. (*High voice.*) Don't call me dung face, you cow-lover. (*HE begins punching his left head with his right arm and then his right head with his left arm—the heads bounce back*

*like punching bags. HE falls to the ground and begins
wrestling with himself.)*

DR. SLAWKENBERGIUS. Now, let us use this table
top to represent the earth as flat, the way God made it, and
let us use this head—(*MARIA has brought a head on a
tray.)*—to represent for a moment a ridiculous and absurd
rounded earth model. Now, I take this pomegranate—
(*Brought to him by the CROCODILE GIRL in the mouth
of her hand puppet, which kisses him.*) This represents a
small, fat person. What happens if we place the
pomegranate on the flat earth model like so?

*(HE puts the pomegranate on the table. The MAD FOLK
look on breathlessly.)*

DR. SLAWKENBERGIUS. Nothing.

(The MAD FOLK applaud and cheer.)

DR. SLAWKENBERGIUS. The pomegranate goes
about it's business in perfect peace and contentment. But
now look what happens when we place this same happy
and unsuspecting pomegranate on this rounded earth
model—(*To the head, which he has in one hand.*) All right?
(*Low voice, as the HEAD answering.*) All right. (*To the
pomegranate, which HE has picked up in the other hand.*)
You are not afraid? (*High voice, as the POMEGRANATE.*)
I am not afraid. (*His own voice.*) You're a good boy. Now.
Observe carefully. (*HE puts the head on the table, and
places the pomegranate on top of the head. It rolls off.*

High voice of the terrified POMEGRANATE.)
Ahhhhhhhhhhhh.

(The MAD FOLK scream and hide their faces.)

DR. SLAWKENBERGIUS. (*His own voice.*) There.
You see? It rolls off. Now, I ask you, my friend, to listen
to the voice of scientific experiment and reason. If the earth
were in fact round, like certain demented persons assert,
would we have any pomegranates left? Answer me that,
HAH? HA HA? Answer me that. Go on. You can't, can
you?

COLUMBUS. Excuse me, but I was just looking for—

DR. SLAWKENBERGIUS. You ARE the crazy Italian
who wants to go east by sailing west, aren't you?

COLUMBUS. Yes, but—

DR. SLAWKENBERGIUS Well, let's look into the
logic of that. By following this same line of reasoning, if I
am in Amsterdam, say, and I wish to visit Poland, I must
first go to France. You must have a terrible time finding
your way to the shithouse in the morning. Do you poop in
the kitchen? And think of your poor wife, sir.

COLUMBUS. I have no wife.

DR. SLAWKENBERGIUS. And it's no wonder, with
all that poop in your kitchen. Am I to believe that
whenever you wish, on a given night, to enter privily into
your wife's eastern parts, you turn the poor woman over
and try to get there by ramming your mizzenmast into her
western parts? This must be very confusing for her.

ANCIENT MARINER. (*A rather formidable looking
old sailor, to Slawkenbergius.*) Go away.

DR. SLAWKENBERGIUS. But I am merely trying to help this poor unfortunate madman see that—

ANCIENT MARINER. (*Growling and barking like a ferocious dog.*) Grrr. Rowrl rowrl rowrllllll. ARRR. RUFFF. RRRRRUFF.

(*SLAWKENBERGIUS scurries off with head and pomegranate, JUANA swiping the latter.*)

ANCIENT MARINER. Don't mind him. He has mental problems. I'm the Ancient Mariner. What do you want with me?

COLUMBUS. I heard from some sailors that you were many years ago on a ship that sailed far west into the great Ocean Sea.

ANCIENT MARINER. So?

COLUMBUS. Can you tell me what you found there?

ANCIENT MARINER. Why?

COLUMBUS. Because I'd like to sail there, too.

ANCIENT MARINER. Are you insane?

COLUMBUS. I want to find an ocean route to China.

ANCIENT MARINER. Iceland.

COLUMBUS. No, China.

ANCIENT MARINER. We set out from Iceland. That's where the legends are. Leif the Lucky went to Vinland. Olga Schmolga went to Finland. Four, five hundred years ago.

COLUMBUS. And he sailed west?

ANCIENT MARINER. (*Crossing his arms and pointing in both directions.*) That way.

COLUMBUS. How far did he sail?

ANCIENT MARINER. (*Measuring about two feet with his hands.*) Oh, about this far, on the map. Or is that how long my willy is? Been so long since I've used it for anything important, I've forgotten.

COLUMBUS. Could he have gone to China?

ANCIENT MARINER. Called it Vinland.

COLUMBUS. Was there an Emperor?

ANCIENT MARINER. There was trees. Grapes. And Skraelings. Killed a bunch.

COLUMBUS. What are Skraelings? Animals?

ANCIENT MARINER. I don't know, I wasn't there, and I'm half blind, anyway, that's how I can see. Why do you care?

COLUMBUS. I want to go there, to China. I believe Vinland was northern China.

ANCIENT MARINER. Watch out you don't go blind, you might accidentally find what you were looking for, although I doubt it, seems like you're going in the wrong direction, but maybe that's the best way. Me, I'm looking for a good pair of Swedish tits.

COLUMBUS. But you sailed west yourself, didn't you?

ANCIENT MARINER. That's where I found them. Not Swedish tits. A man and a woman, clinging to a log, in the middle of the sea, naked as Adam and Eve, with strange eyes, delicate people, her with long black hair and not ashamed of her nakedness, loveliest arms and legs, Lord. We sent out the dinghy and pulled them in, spoke some kind of gibberish we couldn't make head nor tail of, though we had a ship full of sailors been everyplace. Most beautiful woman I ever hope to see, like a dream, dark, sad eyes. The man died first. She was stronger, but after a bit

she died, too. We wrapped them in blankets and dumped
'em in the ocean. And I've never before nor since heard no
language sounded like theirs, nor seen any woman half that
lovely. I was a boy then, I'm old now, half blind, in a
madhouse, but I still dream about her. Her eyes.

COLUMBUS. Were they Skraelings?

ANCIENT MARINER. They was mermaid people,
from Atlantis, and they drowned in the air. Come to the
surface by mistake, swum in the wrong direction, like you,
and the air drowned 'em.

TORQUEMADA. These are the fruits of lunacy.

JUANA. No, actually, it's a pomegranate, do you want
some? It's very good. (*Holds out the pomegranate to
Torquemada, and addresses him in high voice, as
pomegranate:*) Eat me, eat me.

TORQUEMADA. Get away, get away.

7 (Courtship)

COLUMBUS *is pounced on by DIRTY CARLOS and
dragged to the bedroom where MONIZ waits with
FELIPA and the NURSE.*

COLUMBUS. Hey. What is this? Stop that. I'm a
citizen of Genoa and a Christian. Let me go, I'd prefer not
to hurt you.

MONIZ. You are a filthy, slime-devouring ground slug.

COLUMBUS. Now listen here. There's no need to be
unpleasant. Just who do you think you are?

MONIZ. I am the sworn guardian of the innocent young creature you've seduced and gotten with child.

COLUMBUS. Oh. I see. Well. Um. First shot a bull's eye, huh? I'm fairly ignorant of the customs here in Portugal. What is the usual punishment for this sort of thing?

NURSE. Do you have dismemberment insurance?

MONIZ. As much as I would enjoy roasting you on a spit, in this case, much to my regret, it means that my niece is going to make an unfortunate and hasty marriage.

COLUMBUS. Sir, I will never marry under compulsion. That would be an insult to your niece. However, if this extremely surly individual would unhand me for a moment, I might of my own free will ask this beautiful young lady if she would consent to marry me.

MONIZ. Ask her from where you are.

COLUMBUS. All right. Felipa, would you do me the great honor of becoming my wife?

FELIPA. No.

COLUMBUS. No?

FELIPA. No, I said NO. No.

MONIZ. Well, then, we'll just have to kill him.

COLUMBUS. WAIT. Felipa, I thought you loved me.

FELIPA. Where have you been?

COLUMBUS. I went to the madhouse.

FELIPA. For two months?

COLUMBUS. Well, I had a little trouble getting in, and a lot of trouble getting out. I tried a hundred times to see you, but Mister Personality here was guarding the house. Ask him. Can he talk?

(DIRTY CARLOS whacks him in the head.)

COLUMBUS. Ahhhhhhh.

FELIPA. In that case, although I do not consent to marry you, I might allow you to court me.

MONIZ. Make it quick.

COLUMBUS. I would be delighted to court you for several days and then marry you before I go to Iceland.

FELIPA. Iceland? You're going to Iceland?

TORQUEMADA. You abandoned your pregnant wife and went to Iceland?

JUANA. It was their honeymoon. They needed ice.

COLUMBUS. It was to confirm the old sailor's story. I came back to her, and her uncle set us up on an island in the Atlantic, where we lived happily together for some time.

8 (Island)

BIRD sounds. Ocean. COLUMBUS and FELIPA on their island, looking out over the water.

FELIPA. Are you sorry you married me?

COLUMBUS. I'm delighted I married you.

FELIPA. Do you hate this island, then?

COLUMBUS. I like this island very much. This is the calmest my brain has ever been in my life.

FELIPA. But you seem so preoccupied all the time.

COLUMBUS. I'm learning. I watch the ocean. I study the charts. I look at the sky and try to understand the weather. I make maps. I know when it's going to rain. I keep track of the winds. I talk to all the sailors who pass by on ships and learn where they've been and what they've seen. And I have you, and our little boy. This is a very good time in my life.

FELIPA. Then why do you want it to end?

COLUMBUS. I don't want it to end. But it will, I can't stop it. Nothing lasts forever but death.

FELIPA. Is that what you've been having nightmares about? Death?

COLUMBUS. Have I been having nightmares?

FELIPA. Every night. So have I. In my nightmares you're always drowned or shipwrecked, lost at sea.

COLUMBUS. That's not going to happen. I'm a very lucky man. I always have been.

FELIPA. Then what are you always thinking about?

COLUMBUS. A sailor told me about the Vivaldi brothers. They tried to sail west, to see what was out there, at the other side of the ocean sea, and they never came back. I wonder what happened to them? And what did they see before it happened? Is their experience lost forever? Or does God have it somewhere in a book I could open and read? Does time swallow up all truths? There must be a book in which all truth is written, all private experience, everything thought by those who did not say, and those who were never heard from again. I want to read that book.

FELIPA. (*Pulling him towards the bed.*) I want to go to bed and make love. Then you can go to sleep and have more nightmares. I think you like your nightmares more than me.

COLUMBUS. (*Letting himself be pulled into bed.*) I don't like anything more than you.

TORQUEMADA. Clearly these nightmares were sent by the Devil to torment and ensnare this man's soul.

JUANA. No, no, they were messages from God, pages from his book, written in code, in the mysterious code of God's logbook. Trust me, I know about these things, God and I are very close, we play checkers. It's true. He cheats.

(*THUNDER, as if God is not pleased with this comment, and a storm brews—*)

9 (Nightmare)

THUNDER and LIGHTNING. The stage DARKENS ominously, a WINDSTORM whips the tattered sails of the shipwreck. COLUMBUS and FELIPA snuggled together in bed. The VIVALDI BROTHERS appear upstage of the bed and converge on it. THEY are dead and green, in tattered clothing, trailing seaweed.

FIRST VIVALDI. Is that him?

SECOND VIVALDI. I think that's him. Is that his wife? What a cutie. Lucky guy.

FIRST VIVALDI. We should wake him up. Touch his neck.

SECOND VIVALDI. You touch his neck, I'll touch his wife.

FIRST VIVALDI. I'll touch his neck.

(HE touches Columbus on the neck. COLUMBUS jumps up, looks at them, leaps back in terror. FELIPA stirs but does not wake up.)

COLUMBUS. Ahhh. What was that? Who are you? What are you doing in my bedroom?

SECOND VIVALDI. Admiring your wife. Nice hair.

COLUMBUS. Get away from her. What do you want with me?

FIRST VIVALDI. We are the Vivaldi brothers. I am one, and he is the other one. We sailed west a hundred years ago into the vast ocean sea and vanished into God's logbook.

COLUMBUS. Really? And what did you find? What happened to you?

FIRST VIVALDI. We were eaten by sea monsters.

SECOND VIVALDI. We fell off the edge of the world.

FIRST VIVALDI. We were sucked to death by vampire mermaids.

SECOND VIVALDI. We were taken to Atlantis and dissected by scientists.

FIRST VIVALDI. We were hypnotized by the sun.

SECOND VIVALDI. We were devoured by ravenous seagulls.

FIRST VIVALDI. We sailed into the mouth of Satan and were swallowed.

SECOND VIVALDI. We found China, married Chinese women, who are very accomplished at all forms of sexual intercourse, became fabulously wealthy, and were then castrated and torn into twelve equal parts by jealous Mandarins.

FIRST VIVALDI. We fell asleep and never woke up.

SECOND VIVALDI. We're still sailing, we'll sail forever, on a sea that never ends.

COLUMBUS. But which is it? Which is true?

FIRST VIVALDI. All of the above.

SECOND VIVALDI. None of the above.

FIRST VIVALDI. Some are true and some are false.

COLUMBUS. But how do I know which is which?

SECOND VIVALDI. The ones that are not false are true, except for the ones that are partly true, and these are of course also partly false, depending on where your horse happens to squat.

COLUMBUS. But I want to know for certain.

FIRST VIVALDI. The need for certainty is a dangerous form of madness. You will be punished for this.

SECOND VIVALDI. You will be eaten by barnacles.

FIRST VIVALDI. You will be sucked up by sponges.

(COLUMBUS hides under the covers.)

SECOND VIVALDI. You will be devoured by God.

FIRST VIVALDI. You will be eviscerated by schoolchildren.

SECOND VIVALDI. You will drown in your own illusions.

BOTH VIVALDIS. You will become—history.

COLUMBUS. (*Sitting up in bed, crying out.*) NO. NOT THAT. NO.

FELIPA. (*Waking up, bleary eyed, as the VIVALDIS disappear into the darkened shipwreck.*) What? Who are you talking to?

COLUMBUS. This is a sign. It's a sign.

FELIPA. You had a nightmare. Go back to sleep.

COLUMBUS. No, it's a sign from God that I must stop wallowing in uncertainty and take action. I will go and see Prince John of Portugal. (*HE starts getting dressed.*)

FELIPA. (*Trying to pull him back into bed.*) No. Stay here with me.

COLUMBUS. But he's an intelligent man, he'll give me ships to sail west in, then I'll find the truth, and I'll be rich and famous. People will love me.

FELIPA. But I love you NOW.

COLUMBUS. Yes, but people I don't KNOW will love me. I will be respected. Don't you see? I will be a great man.

FELIPA. Christopher—

COLUMBUS. I will be a great man.

10 (The Portuguese Court)

Immediately the HONK HONK of the JESTER's horn, which HE blows directly in Christopher's ear, startling and disorienting him, and we are at the court of PRINCE JOHN of Portugal, a dark, sardonic man. His court, disturbingly enough, seems to be made up of mad people, the PIG WOMAN, DESDEMONA, MARIA, the CROCODILE GIRL and the CROW WOMAN.

PRINCE JOHN. So? What is it? What do you want from me?

COLUMBUS. Your majesty, I am overwhelmed by your generosity in seeing me about this issue which is of profound importance to the history of your nation, and, if I may say so, to the history of mankind as a whole. All the world knows of your interest in exploration and discovery—

(The JESTER honks his horn again, HONK HONK.)

PRINCE JOHN. Let's try to condense the sucking up, all right? We have established that I am great and wonderful and that you are obsequious vermin, now, what is it you want?

COLUMBUS. I want a ship to sail west to China.

JESTER. (*Bursting out in hysterical laughter.*) HAW HAW HAW HEE HEEEEE—(*HE puts his hand to his mouth and stops himself.*)

PRINCE JOHN. You mean east.

COLUMBUS. No, west. I've made calculations that demonstrate conclusively that if one sails directly west from Portugal one will in a few days at most reach the coasts of China—

PRINCE JOHN Have we checked these calculations? Where is the expert?

JESTER. (*Presenting him with grand arm gesture.*) DA DAHHHHHH.

DR. SLAWKENBERGIUS. (*Jumping out suddenly from behind Columbus.*) Yes, your excellency, I am the world's greatest authority, and I have checked and rechecked this man's calculations.

COLUMBUS. Wait a minute. I know you. You're the one who—

DR. SLAWKENBERGIUS. I am sorry to report that this imbecile has grossly underestimated the circumference of the earth.

COLUMBUS. The last time I saw you, you said the earth was flat.

DR. SLAWKENBERGIUS. I've never seen this man before in my life. Not only is he a terrible mathematician, he's delusional. If he sails west, the journey to China should take at least four times as long as he's estimated. If there's no land between here and there, he'll run out of food and water long before he gets there. And the extreme stupidity of his calculations leads me to suspect that this man is both unstable and unscrupulous, either immensely incompetent or a juggler of figures for his own purposes, or some unwholesome combination of the two. We definitely recommend NO. Sorry, and have a nice day.

COLUMBUS. Just who IS this person, to be calling me names?

DR. SLAWKENBERGIUS. I am the world's greatest authority.

COLUMBUS. And who decided that?

DR. SLAWKENBERGIUS. I did.

COLUMBUS. And what gives you that right?

DR. SLAWKENBERGIUS. Because I'm the world's greatest authority, you doorknob, what have you got, pudding in your ears?

PRINCE JOHN. I think you'd better stick to making maps, my confused Italian friend, go home and sleep with your wife. You may investigate her unknown regions with greater pleasure and much less expense.

(The COURT begins laughing.)

COLUMBUS. How dare you laugh at me. How dare you make jokes about my wife. I assure you, I am NOT funny.

(The JESTER runs up and smashes a pie directly in Christopher's face. The COURT bursts into wild laughter. A whole stage full of maniacally laughing PEOPLE are pointing at him. The JESTER trips him. HE falls on his face. As HE gets up, the JESTER pulls down his pants and pushes him over again, foot to rump. The PEOPLE are in animal hysterics. JUANA rushes over, pushes the Jester away, and with her handkerchief helps COLUMBUS wipe the pie off his face.)

COLUMBUS. (*Going home, humiliated and furious, wiping his face.*) Why should I degrade myself begging in front of morons? Why should their laughter trouble me? The contempt of fools is a badge of honor. If cretins despise you it proves you're not one of them. All I want to do is go home and make love to my wife. That's all I need.

Just to lie naked in bed in the arms of my wife at night in the dark and feel her heart beating against me, her breath on my face, smell her hair, know that one creature in the world is warm and happy and safe because I exist. That's all there is. The hell with everything else.

11 (Death)

A BELL tolls. Upstage by the bed, the NURSE crying at the bed where FELIPA lies. TORQUEMADA prays over her. JUANA goes up to look.

MONIZ. (*Stopping Columbus downstage.*) Wait. Don't go in yet.

COLUMBUS. Señor Moniz, how nice to see you. I didn't know you were coming to visit us. Felipa must have been so happy to have you here while I was away.

MONIZ. I said, don't go in.

COLUMBUS. Why not? It's my house. Well, it's YOUR house, but, I mean, it's my wife's house, and I live there. What's wrong? You haven't taken her away somewhere, have you?

MONIZ. Your wife is dead.

COLUMBUS. That's ridiculous. I've only been away for a few weeks. She was perfectly fine when I left. She stood right there and kissed me goodbye. What are you saying?

MONIZ. I'm saying that while her husband was off making a fool of himself in Lisbon, my beautiful child died, alone, on an island, abandoned by him. She's gone. God has taken her.

COLUMBUS. This is another one of those nightmares, isn't it? All right, I'm going to wake up now. I'm going to count three and then wake up in bed with my wife. I need to touch my wife. My wife. I need my wife.

TORQUEMADA. You married this girl because her family had money, ships, maps and an island in the Atlantic. Why make a mockery of her death by pretending grief you didn't feel?

COLUMBUS. I did feel it. I loved my wife.

TORQUEMADA. Then you should have been happy she went to heaven to be with God.

COLUMBUS. But God didn't need her. I did.

TORQUEMADA. Blasphemy.

COLUMBUS. She was just a child. The grief surprised me. When she was taken from me it was a horrible shock to realize how much I had come to depend upon her love. I had never allowed myself to depend on any person in the past. A woman was a miraculous creature to be chased and won, enjoyed and then—one went on with one's life. To lose her was—I couldn't bear it. And so, I did what any good Christian would do.

JUANA. You prayed to God for understanding.

COLUMBUS. Yes. And when that didn't work, I got stinking drunk.

12 (Ghost)

MARIA brings him a bottle. HE drinks.

COLUMBUS. (*Wandering with bottle.*) The world is flat and dead. I am spat upon by cretins. I've murdered my wife.

FELIPA. *(In white, looking very nice.)* That's the stupidest thing I've ever heard. You didn't kill me. God killed me. You were just an innocent bystander.

COLUMBUS. Felipa?

FELIPA. Now stop all this self-pity right now, it's beneath you, really, and get on with things. Life is short, I should know, mine certainly was.

COLUMBUS. You're not dead.

FELIPA. Of course I'm dead, but that doesn't mean I have no opinions. Now, stop drinking and take care of our son, he needs you. And go to Spain.

COLUMBUS. Spain? What's in Spain?

FELIPA. I haven't the slightest idea. Bulls, I think. But I've been to Heaven and snuck a look at the book of possible futures perhaps, and it says that if you go to Spain, you'll find what you're looking for.

COLUMBUS. You're really dead?

FELIPA. Well, I no longer feel any need to pee. I can appear or disappear more or less at will. And I've just been playing pinochle with Julius Caesar and Moses. Either I'm dead or one of us is losing it in a big way.

COLUMBUS. It's me. I'm going insane.

FELIPA. You're not going insane. You were born insane. Just stop crying in cheap wine and put your particular brand of insanity to some use before you, too, lose your capacity to urinate, will you do that for me?

COLUMBUS. Yes. I will.

FELIPA. You promise?

COLUMBUS. I swear.

FELIPA. That's my good boy. What a good boy you are. Don't forget me too soon.

COLUMBUS. Never. I never will.

FELIPA. (*Touching his face sadly.*) The living are so innocent. And such liars.

TORQUEMADA. Clearly another visitation from the Devil.

COLUMBUS. It was not the Devil, it was my dead wife.

TORQUEMADA. May I remind you that I hold a very high position in organized religion? If I don't know the Devil when I see him, who does? So, the Devil told you to go to Spain.

COLUMBUS. My dead wife told me to go to Spain. But when I got there, I hadn't the slightest idea what to do.

13 (Here We Are in Sunny Spain)

Guitar MUSIC. COLUMBUS at an inn in Spain, staring at a full glass. DIEGO drinks nearby with DESDEMONA. DIRTY CARLOS is the bartender, MARIA, the serving girl. THEY all stare at Columbus.

DIEGO. Go on, drink it.

COLUMBUS. I beg your pardon?

DIEGO. You come into this inn, you order a drink, and then you sit and stare at it for three hours, as if you were afraid it was going to grow legs and run away.

COLUMBUS. I'm trying to figure out how to see the Queen.

DESDEMONA. You think she's in your glass?

DIEGO. Why do you want to see the Queen?

COLUMBUS. You'll laugh at me if I tell you.

DIEGO. I promise not to laugh. Tell me, what can it hurt?

COLUMBUS. I want her to give me a boat.

DIEGO. I see.

COLUMBUS. So I can sail west to China.

DIEGO. Ummm. Well, that's a tough one. I can see why you're depressed.

COLUMBUS. I'm depressed because I've betrayed my wife.

DIEGO. That's happened a few times in the history of the world. Be a man, get on your knees and beg. She'll forgive you. Kiss her feet. Kiss her private parts.

COLUMBUS. I can't kiss her private parts, she's in Portugal. And she's dead.

DIEGO. She's dead in Portugal and you've betrayed her?

COLUMBUS. Yes.

DIEGO. Why don't you drink your beer? Maybe if we're both drunk, we can understand each other better.

COLUMBUS. I can't. I promised my wife.

DIEGO. Who is dead in Portugal.

COLUMBUS. Who is dead in Portugal, yes.

DIEGO. But if you promised your wife, who is dead, not to drink, and you're not drinking, then—

COLUMBUS. I've betrayed her by having many lustful thoughts.

DIEGO. You mean that counts?

COLUMBUS. And now, to punish me, she's stopped coming to see me.

DIEGO. Your wife who is dead has stopped coming to see you?

COLUMBUS. Yes.

DIEGO. Listen, my friend, I wouldn't take that personally. Dead people are very busy.

COLUMBUS. But she used to come and comfort me, and give me advice. She told me to come to Spain.

DIEGO. When she was dead?

COLUMBUS. Exactly. But now she won't talk to me, since I began having lustful thoughts.

DIEGO. What you need, my friend, is a good—

(HE looks across the stage to where BEATRIZ is getting into bed, and has a happy thought.)

DIEGO. —a good meal. Yes, a home cooked meal. Come home with me, and my beautiful cousin Beatriz will cook you a wonderful meal. Come on. No objections. You'll feel much better, I guarantee it.

COLUMBUS. Thank you, sir, but I really couldn't—

DIEGO. (Pulling Columbus away towards the bedroom.) Diego. And yes you can. (HE goes back and drinks Columbus's drink.) Spain is a very friendly country. And my cousin is a very friendly girl.

TORQUEMADA. So this man Diego took you, a complete stranger, into his home?

COLUMBUS. (*Taking his pants off.*) Spain is a very friendly country.

TORQUEMADA. And then what?

COLUMBUS. And I woke up in the morning with a terrible headache.

14 (Beatriz)

COLUMBUS holds his head and staggers in the room of Beatriz, morning.

COLUMBUS. Oh. Ohhhhh. I feel like a squashed roach. (*HE stumbles back to the bed, where HE pulls back the covers to find BEATRIZ.*) Felipa? You're not Felipa.

BEATRIZ. I'm Beatriz, silly.

COLUMBUS. Who?

BEATRIZ. Beatriz, the cousin of Diego.

COLUMBUS. Who?

BEATRIZ. Diego, who brought you home to dinner and convinced you to drink his homemade wine.

COLUMBUS. Oh, God, I've betrayed my wife.

BEATRIZ. Your wife is dead. You told me all about her. You told me, in fact, nearly everything there was to tell in the entire world, since the beginning of creation. And I said to myself, Beatriz, this is a man who talks all the time who hasn't said anything in months. It was like puncturing a gourd. You talked about sailing west to get to

China, about your wife, Marco Polo, Pliny the Elder, mermaids and the Queen of Spain.

COLUMBUS. I'm very sorry to have bored you with all that.

BEATRIZ. Oh, but I found you immensely charming. Otherwise I certainly wouldn't have let you sleep with me.

COLUMBUS. Oh, GOD, this keeps happening to me. You must forgive me, it's not my fault, I'm Italian.

BEATRIZ. Listen, maybe I can help you. A good friend of mine has a position at court—

(We see ROSAURA chased by BOBADILLA at court.)

BEATRIZ. —and she's a friend of the Marquesa de Moya—

(We see the MARQUESA intercept BOBADILLA.)

BEATRIZ. —who's a very close friend of the Queen.

COLUMBUS. You can get me in to see the Queen?

BEATRIZ. No, but I think I can get you introduced to the Marquesa, and if she likes you, and you talk a great deal, she might perhaps get you a royal audience.

COLUMBUS. What did you say your name was?

BEATRIZ. Beatriz.

COLUMBUS. Beatriz, I am deeply in love with you.

BEATRIZ. I certainly hope so.

TORQUEMADA. So you met with this friend of your new whore?

COLUMBUS. Beatriz was not a whore, she was a fine woman.

TORQUEMADA. And you also, how shall I put it, charmed her friend?

COLUMBUS. Certainly not. (*HE looks at ROSAURA, who smiles.*) Well, actually, yes. And she introduced me to the Marquesa de Moya.

TORQUEMADA. And did you charm her as well?

COLUMBUS. (*Exchanging a glance with the MARQUESA.*) Only a few times, but it was, I assure you, ultimately for the greater glory of God, as he in his wisdom inspired her to get me admitted to the presence of the King and Queen of Spain.

15 (The Spanish Court)

The JESTER blows his horn as fanfare.

JESTER. Their royal majesties, King Ferdinand and Queen Isabella. (*HE blows the horn again.*)

FERDINAND. (*Cranky like the King of Spades.*) Will you stop it with the damn horn? Where did we get this fool, anyway? Why can't we get good help? Who are you?

COLUMBUS. Cristoforo Colombo, your majesty, and let me begin by saying what a great honor it is for me to be here and—

FERDINAND. Yes, yes, we know, just get to the point.

COLUMBUS. I have a project which I believe—

FERDINAND. This means you want money. Project equals money. There are certain code words you become familiar with when you rule by divine right.

COLUMBUS. For centuries, scholars have pondered the question, voiced by Pliny the Elder and others—

FERDINAND. You've got ten seconds to tell me exactly what you want or get the hell out of here.

COLUMBUS. I want a boat so I can sail west to China.

FERDINAND. You don't need a boat, you need a map. China's in the east.

COLUMBUS. But the world being, as most learned men of our time agree, a sphere, then if one sails west, on the great Ocean Sea, one must eventually come back to the east.

FERDINAND. Thank you for your suggestion. We'll get back to you. Now if you'll excuse me, I've had a rough day.

COLUMBUS. But your majesty—

FERDINAND. Good night.

ISABELLA. We might at least do him the courtesy—

FERDINAND. You do him the courtesy, it was your idea to see this crackpot in the first place. I'm going to bed.

(HE starts away. The JESTER blows the horn in his ear. FERDINAND rips it from his hands.)

FERDINAND. Give me that damned thing. (*HE whacks the Jester over the head with it.*) Get out of here. Get.

(HE chases the Jester out. COLUMBUS and ISABELLA look at each other.)

ISABELLA. So you're a friend of the Marquesa de Moya?

COLUMBUS. I have the honor to have made her acquaintance.

ISABELLA. Yes, she told me all about it.

COLUMBUS. *(Nervously looking at the Marquesa.)* Did she?

ISABELLA. She says you're a very charming man.

COLUMBUS. She's very kind.

ISABELLA. No she's not. You're Italian, is that right? From Genoa, where they make those large sausages?

COLUMBUS. Fairly large, yes.

ISABELLA. Don't you have a wife back in Genoa who misses you?

COLUMBUS. My wife was Portuguese, but she's dead.

ISABELLA I'm sorry. I would think that a man like you—

ROSAURA. *(Running in, scantily clad, screaming.)* AAAAHHHH. AHHHHHHHHHH. *(Bumping into Columbus.)* Oh, hello Christopher.

JUANA. *(Chasing her with a large pair of shears.)* SLUT. SLIME. FORNICATRESS!

ROSAURA. HELP. HELP ME. MURDER.

(SHE grabs onto Columbus and uses him as a shield as the enraged JUANA circles them.)

JUANA. Get out from behind that man or I'll cut my way through him.

ISABELLA. Juana, put that down this instant.

JUANA. I'll put it down, in this slut's right eye socket.

ROSAURA. Your majesty, please help me, your daughter is insane again, she's going to slaughter me like a pig.

JUANA. You ARE a pig.

ISABELLA. Juana, stop it.

JUANA. It's all right, Mama, I was just out trimming a few sluts, and since this woman is the biggest slut in Europe, I thought I'd start with her, conveniently located as she was, in my bed, underneath my husband.

ROSAURA. AHHHHHHHHHH. (*SHE avoids a lunge and hides behind the Queen.*)

ISABELLA. GUARD. GUARD. Oh, they're off humping the chambermaids again.

COLUMBUS. Allow me. (*HE snatches the shears from Juana.*)

JUANA. You give me those back or I'll kill you. I will. I'm a Spanish princess, I can do anything I want.

ISABELLA. Juana, a young lady does not murder her friends with scissors.

JUANA. Well, I didn't have a gun, and she's not my friend, she copulates with my husband, and who IS this person?

COLUMBUS. Cristoforo Colombo, at your service.

JUANA. Then give me back my shears and get out of my way so I can skin this cow.

ROSAURA. You just keep away from me or I'll tell the king on you. Your majesty? Your majesty? (*SHE runs off after Ferdinand.*)

ISABELLA. Oh, no, don't bother the king, oh dear, excuse me, Mr. Columbia, could you watch over my insane daughter here for a moment while I try and stop this stupid girl from waking up my husband, who will either have her drawn and quartered or else jump on her himself. Thank you. (*SHE goes off after Rosaura.*)

(*Columbus finds himself holding the shears high in the air with one hand while containing the struggling, furious JUANA by the waist and parallel to the floor with the other.*)

JUANA. Take your filthy hands off me.

COLUMBUS. No. Sorry.

JUANA. Nobody says no to me.

COLUMBUS. I think that's part of the problem. I'll let you go if you promise to behave yourself.

JUANA. I don't have to behave myself, I'm royalty.

COLUMBUS. Then start acting like it, and I'll treat you that way.

JUANA. All I want to do is slice open the throat of that melon-breasted sow that took my husband from me. Is that such an unreasonable request?

(*HE lets her get away from him, and SHE sits down in despair, crying and raging.*)

COLUMBUS. I know how you feel. I loved my wife very much, too.

JUANA. Really? Did she sleep with swine?

COLUMBUS. Only me.

JUANA. Then how can you know how I feel?

COLUMBUS. This woman takes your husband like God took my wife, and you feel horrible, angry, powerless, as if it's your fault. I also have a bad temper on occasion. But it did me no good to be angry at God.

JUANA. That hussy is not God.

COLUMBUS. She's God's instrument, and she does God's will.

JUANA. It's God's will that this strumpet should rut with my husband? Boy, what a pervert.

COLUMBUS. Look. God took my wife to be with him in Heaven. He made her, he loved her, he took her. If I lead a reasonably decent life, some day I'll be with her again. All I need is to have a little patience. Your husband sleeps with this young woman once or twice. He's young, she's attractive, it's not right, but people do this. If you have a little patience, he'll forget about her and come back to you, because you're his wife, and a Princess, and very beautiful, and if he's even remotely worth all the love you feel for him, he'll realize that.

JUANA. But I have no patience. I'm insane.

COLUMBUS. Join the club. They think I'm insane, too, because I want to sail west to get to China.

JUANA. Well, yes, but you see, that really IS insane.

COLUMBUS. Nevertheless, that's what I'm going to do.

JUANA. Why?

COLUMBUS. Why do you love your husband?

JUANA. I don't know. I can't explain it.

COLUMBUS. So, there we are, all desire is insane. We're on the earth for a very short time, and we have creatures we love or things we need to do, so we must play out our action, like an actor who knows his lines, and trust that God the playwright knows what he's doing.

JUANA. Does that mean I should go ahead and cut this woman's throat?

COLUMBUS. Why don't you try concentrating on your husband first. You haven't been neglecting him, have you?

JUANA. No. I just haven't slept with him.

COLUMBUS. Never?

JUANA. No. Is that bad?

COLUMBUS. How long have you been married?

JUANA. Six months.

COLUMBUS. Have you considered the possibility that this might have something to do with his behavior with that young lady?

JUANA. You think so? Really? Could be. I'm afraid.

COLUMBUS. There's nothing to be afraid of. When the time comes, you know what to do. And clearly your husband knows what to do. Be brave, and give of yourself. Then this poor pathetic little mistress has no chance at all against you. After all, you're the Princess of Spain, yes?

JUANA. But I'm only a child. I play with dolls. Suck my thumb. I've never been allowed anywhere near a man, and then suddenly I'm supposed to allow him to do the most grotesque and bizarre things to my body. It's impossible. (*SHE starts to cry again.*)

COLUMBUS. Oh, no, no, no, here, here. (*HE holds her.*) It's easy, really. Here. (*Very gently HE kisses her on the lips. Then HE pulls away and smiles at her.*) See?

JUANA. (*Amazed.*) Is that what it feels like?

COLUMBUS. It gets better later on, trust me.

JUANA. Oh. Well, I can do that.

COLUMBUS. I know you can. God has quietly taught us how to do many things we don't know we know how to do until we have the courage to do them.

JUANA. Can we practice some more?

COLUMBUS. I'd love to, but I think perhaps you should practice on your husband.

ISABELLA. (*Returning.*) My God, what a stupid girl. And YOU, Juana, shame on you for behaving like a savage.

JUANA. (*Very civilized.*) Yes, you're right, Mama, I was terribly ill behaved, and I'm very sorry for it. I'm fine now, and I'm going to find my dear husband and discuss this with him like two adults. (*Shaking hands with Columbus very formally.*) Thank you, Mr. Columbus, I've enjoyed our little talk more than I can say, and I hope that my Mama will give you whatever you want. Goodbye. Goodbye, Mama. (*SHE gives Isabella a dainty kiss on the cheek, and starts out, ISABELLA thoroughly bewildered by this transformation. Then JUANA stops and turns, still smiling radiantly:*) But if she ever tries it again—(*Making a cutting motion across her throat.*) Zzzzzzzzzzzzpppp. (*SHE bounces off happily.*)

ISABELLA. How in God's name did you manage to do that?

COLUMBUS. We talked.

ISABELLA. I've been trying with little or no success to talk to that girl for most of her life.

COLUMBUS. A stranger is sometimes easier.

ISABELLA. Well, it seems I owe you a favor. You want to sail west to China. Why should I care?

COLUMBUS. Because a safe, quick sea route to the Orient would make Spain the richest nation in the world.

ISABELLA. You're Italian, why do you want to make Spain rich?

COLUMBUS. I don't. If I fail here, I'll go to England or France. I just want to sail west to get to the east.

ISABELLA. But why devote your life to such an insane idea?

COLUMBUS. Because I know it can be done.

ISABELLA. And I know that sword-swallowing and fire-eating can be done, but I don't want to spend my life sticking flaming swords down my throat. I need a better reason. Come on, no rhetoric and no tricks. Why do you want to do this?

COLUMBUS. Have you never walked into a room and, confronted unexpectedly by some person or some place or thing, known instantly that you were looking at the rest of your life? I've had such an experience. I've looked out over the ocean sea and seen my future there, as if painted in God's picture book. It was like a voice had spoken to me, it was very clear.

ISABELLA. So you hear voices, do you? This may explain why you communicate so well with my daughter, who has long conversations with horses and flowers.

COLUMBUS. I can do this. All I need is a ship. Maybe two. Three would be nice, although a fleet would be preferable, since—

ISABELLA. Nobody's going to give you a fleet of anything. It might be possible to find you a ship or two.

COLUMBUS. If you do, it will be the most important thing you ever do, and if you don't, it will be the greatest mistake of your life.

ISABELLA. (*Bursting out laughing.*) Will it?

COLUMBUS. I didn't realize I'd said anything funny. I did not come here to be laughed at. Excuse me. (*HE turns and starts to go.*)

ISABELLA. I don't mean to offend you, really, it's just that you're so dreadfully serious about it. Wait a minute.

(*HE keeps going. SHE stands up. Very different tone, harsh, powerful, this is the Queen speaking.*)

ISABELLA. JUST STOP RIGHT THERE.

(*HE stops.*)

ISABELLA. One does not leave the presence of a sovereign until one has been excused. You must not confuse the present disorder of my court with any weakness or slackness of purpose on either my part or the King's. I've been easy and friendly with you because you're an easy and friendly sort of person, mostly, and rather charming, when you're not getting your feathers ruffled, and you've been useful in a difficult domestic situation. This does not mean you are permitted to forget for one moment who you are, or who I am, is that clear?

COLUMBUS. Yes, your majesty.

ISABELLA. Now get back over here.

(HE comes stiffly back and kneels down formally on one knee before her.)

ISABELLA. Oh, get up, don't be a jackass, I don't want you to fawn over me. Get up.

(HE stands up, still cold.)

ISABELLA. You're a very touchy fellow, aren't you?

COLUMBUS. I've been laughed at by persons in authority before.

ISABELLA. Oh? Anybody I know?

COLUMBUS. Prince John of Portugal, for one.

ISABELLA. Yes, well, he's a pretty cold fish, but he's not stupid.

COLUMBUS. In this case he was.

ISABELLA. You're an arrogant man.

COLUMBUS. I'm a man driven by an obsession. It's such people who get things done in this world. They're laughed at and spat upon and ridiculed by small-minded cretins, but they are, in the end, the people who matter.

ISABELLA. Then you'd better get used to being laughed at and learn not to take it so much to heart. Obsessions are neither good nor evil in themselves, it depends on what you're obsessed with. Talk to me about

yours. If I like what I hear, I'll see what I can do. Well?
Talk.

16 (Ferdinand the Bull)

*As the obsequious BOBADILLA, who has been
eavesdropping, reports to the King.*

TORQUEMADA. And so you talked. All night, I
believe.

COLUMBUS. I had a lot to say.

TORQUEMADA. And the Queen became interested in
your obsession?

FERDINAND. (*Storming over to Isabella, furious, as
JUANA and the court observe and COLUMBUS goes back
to Beatriz.*) You what? You did what?

ISABELLA. I set up a little commission of experts to
study that nice Italian sailor's claims. Don't pop your royal
codpiece, they're already on the payroll, it'll give them
something to do for a change.

FERDINAND. What a monumental waste of time.

ISABELLA. Not if he happens to be right.

FERDINAND. The man's insane.

JUANA. So? What's your point?

FERDINAND. Juana, stay out of this.

ISABELLA. He's not insane, he's merely obsessed.

FERDINAND. Never, never trust an obsessed man. I
hate all obsessive people, they're very dangerous. He'll
stop at nothing, no matter what it costs me. Stay up all

night talking to such people if it amuses you, but never under any circumstances give them any of my money.

ISABELLA. I think what I love about you is your sense of adventure.

FERDINAND. If you want adventures, take a lover, don't spend my money.

ISABELLA. It's MY money.

FERDINAND. No, you never spend YOUR money, you just spend MINE.

ISABELLA. You wouldn't mind if I took a lover?

FERDINAND. I didn't say I wouldn't mind, I said it'd be an adventure. One must keep in mind when embarking upon adventures that all adventures end badly, although some do manage to seem enjoyable in retrospect, but even this requires a great deal of self-deception and more than a little willful stupidity. An adventure in retrospect was a nightmare while it was happening. The survivors comfort themselves with lies.

ISABELLA. So I can take a lover as long as I'm resigned to the fact that it will end badly and only be fun in retrospect?

FERDINAND. You can take a lover if you don't mind one whose sexual equipment and head have been removed.

ISABELLA. And your warmth. I love your warmth.

FERDINAND. If you're looking for warmth, try your confessor Torquemada, he incinerates people who have adventures. Now you'll have to excuse me, I've got some death warrants to sign.

ISABELLA. (*Dangerous and cold.*) While you're at it, sign your own.

FERDINAND. (*Stops, checks his temper, looks at Juana.*) I'm in a lot of trouble here, aren't I?

JUANA. You're in deep guano, pop.

FERDINAND. (*Turns back to Isabella.*) I suppose this means you're going to make my life a living hell until I give in and do what you want.

ISABELLA. Oh, I don't care, you just married me for my kingdom.

FERDINAND. Now don't start that again. How did that lunatic get in here in the first place?

ISABELLA. He's a friend of the Marquesa de Moya.

FERDINAND. Oh, great, I'm surprised she got up off her back long enough to introduce you.

ISABELLA. She's a dear friend of mine.

FERDINAND. That woman's legs have been spread apart so often she can no longer ride side-saddle.

ISABELLA. Well, you ought to know.

(*A moment. THEY look at each other. FERDINAND looks at JUANA, who mimes hanging herself.*)

FERDINAND. You would really trust anything of value to a person like that?

ISABELLA. Something of small to moderate value I might not trust with him, for he's not interested in such things, and might well lose them. Something of great value, maybe.

FERDINAND. You'd trust him with a ship?

ISABELLA. I don't have any ships, you've got the ships. If it was my ship, I'd let him board it, to see if he knows what he's doing, and perhaps allow him a short voyage or two. If you were good enough to keep an open mind about this matter, I might even forget to lock my bedroom door tonight.

(SHE gives him a kiss and goes out. HE starts in the opposite direction, stops, changes his mind, and follows her.)

JUANA. *(Trailing after them.)* Can I watch? I'll be quiet, I just want to take notes.

17 (Waiting)

COLUMBUS pacing as BEATRIZ watches from bed.

BEATRIZ. For God's sake stop cracking your knuckles and come to bed.

COLUMBUS. I was not made for waiting. I go to her stupid panel of adjudicators, a collection of pompous cretins with between them not enough brain matter to service a dog, and they blather at me for hours, and then I don't see them for weeks, and I can't get in to see the Queen. They don't say yes, they don't say no, they say come back next week, next month, next year. They scold me, they flatter me, they patronize me. Why must I spend my life at the mercy of cretins?

BEATRIZ. Because cretins like being in charge of things, that's how they punish people with brains. And the

Queen's busy deporting the Jews from Spain and stealing everything they own.

COLUMBUS. That sort of talk will get you roasted like a chicken.

BEATRIZ. I don't care, I think it's a horrible, cruel, stupid and very unChristian thing to do, don't you?

COLUMBUS. If they don't want to leave, they can simply convert.

BEATRIZ. Maybe they don't want to convert. What do YOU know about it?

COLUMBUS. I know about it. My mother's people converted.

BEATRIZ. You're Jewish and you have no compassion for these people?

COLUMBUS. Keep your voice down. I have dead ancestors who used to be Jewish. I'm a Christian. As long as you convert, they don't kill you. I think that's fair. You make choices and you accept the consequences.

BEATRIZ. You never accepted a consequence in your life. You try to keep one step ahead of them. Some day you're going to drown in consequences.

COLUMBUS. I miss the sea. I haven't been to sea in so long. I've been going to sea since I was thirteen. I want the sea.

BEATRIZ. Clearly I don't satisfy you.

COLUMBUS. It isn't you, it's the sea. I can only relate to the land on maps. The place I'm at is never real. You're just the opposite, you're very down to earth. Only the place you've come to rest at this moment is real for you. So theoretically, you and I should never be able to make contact at all. Our realities never touch.

BEATRIZ. Yes but, thank God, all theories are pig flop.

COLUMBUS. All theories are not pig flop.

BEATRIZ. You're right, that's an insult to pigs. Isn't it real to you when we make love?

COLUMBUS. It's like dreaming. Only the journey is real.

BEATRIZ. This is real.

(SHE kisses him, and HE falls over on top of her in bed as BOBADILLA brings a message from the King.)

COLUMBUS. God, what a philosopher you are. You should write this down.

(HE tickles her, SHE giggles and THEY roll around happily on the bed. DIEGO takes the message.)

DIEGO. Um, excuse me. Excuse me.

COLUMBUS. Go away, I'm making certain important investigations into dark, unknown territory. Got you.

(HE grabs BEATRIZ, who squeals and giggles.)

DIEGO. The king regrets to inform you that he will not be able to finance your voyage.

(COLUMBUS sits there, BEATRIZ holding him from behind.)

COLUMBUS. Oh. I see. Well. It's all right. I'm fine. Everything—is fine.

18 (Juana is Bad)

Immediately, a blood-curdling SCREAM as the MARQUESA DE MOYA runs on with her hair hacked off in patches, some bald, chased by JUANA with shears, chased in turn by ISABELLA.

MARQUESA DE MOYA. AHHHHHHHHH. AHHHHHHHHHHH.

JUANA. Wait, I'm not done yet, let me even it out for you.

ISABELLA. (*Pulling Juana back by her dress.*) Juana, you can't cut all the women at court bald just because your husband happens to look at them.

JUANA. I don't see why not. I'm young. I've got the time. She's lucky I've mellowed since I started having sex.

ISABELLA. Why don't you study your Latin instead?

JUANA. Mama, Latin is what drove me insane in the first place.

ISABELLA. Maybe I should call that Italian sailor back to have another talk with you. He seems to be the only one who can make you behave.

JUANA. It's too late for that. Daddy told him to go to hell.

ISABELLA. Your father rejected his request without telling me?

JUANA. He said you were too busy throwing out the Jews and taking their money to notice.

ISABELLA. Oh, he did, did he?

JUANA. Whoops. I wasn't supposed to tell you that. I'm a bad girl. Shame on me. (*SHE giggles wickedly.*)

19 (Columbus Goes to France)

what?

COLUMBUS is packing. BEATRIZ upset.

BEATRIZ. What do you think you're doing?

COLUMBUS. I'm going to France. Maybe the King of France has a brain. I doubt it, but who knows?

BEATRIZ. Oh, don't go to France, it's a terrible place, they speak French there.

COLUMBUS. Of course they speak French, what do you expect them to do? Yodel at each other?

BEATRIZ. But you can't speak French.

COLUMBUS. I'm a sailor, I speak French as well as I speak Spanish.

BEATRIZ. You speak the worst Spanish I've ever heard.

COLUMBUS. I spoke it well enough to seduce you.

BEATRIZ. I was not seduced by your linguistic skills. Although you ARE good with your tongue. Please don't go. At least kiss me goodbye.

COLUMBUS. I'm not done packing yet.

BEATRIZ. Kiss me goodbye first, it might take a while.

(SHE grabs him and kisses him. HE gets involved in spite of himself as BOBADILLA brings Diego a message from the Queen.)

BEATRIZ. Just for a minute. Just for a day or two. Just for three or four weeks.

(THEY are getting desperately entwined and fall onto the bed.)

BEATRIZ. Just until the vernal equinox. Just till leap year.

DIEGO. Um, excuse me.

BEATRIZ. Not now. He's going to France.

DIEGO. But this is important.

COLUMBUS. Not now, you fool, can't you see I'm on my way to France? *(HE turns back hungrily to Beatriz.)*

DIEGO. But the Queen wants to see you immediately.

COLUMBUS. *(Jumping up, dropping the weak and numb Beatriz with a clunk and a bounce below him on the bed.)* Me? The Queen wants to see me? Well, I don't want to see her. Two can play at this game Hah. Me? She wants to see me? Now? After all this? She wants to see ME? *(HE is desperately trying to pull his pants up and is falling all over the place.)* Never. I'll never see her. She wants to see me right now?

DIEGO. Immediately.

COLUMBUS. She's changed her mind. Beatriz, she's changed her MIND. PASTAFAZOOLA, SHE'S CHANGED HER MIND.

BEATRIZ. (*Looking up, weakly.*) Hooray.

20 (The Mad Italian Returns)

The JESTER blows his horn. Court.

JESTER. Hear ye, hear ye—

(*FERDINAND whacks him over the head.*)

JESTER. Ahhhhh. Owwww. Hey.

JUANA. CHRISTOPHER! (*SHE runs up and jumps in his arms.*) Guess what? I had sex with my husband. Sixty-four and a half times. It was great. Well, it was sort of great. Number seventeen was pretty good.

COLUMBUS. (*Putting her down gently.*) Your majesties, I wish to express my gratitude to both of you for finally agreeing to fund my expedition.

FERDINAND. Have you lost your mind? What are you doing here?

ISABELLA. We've said nothing yet about funding you.

FERDINAND. Yes we have. I said no.

COLUMBUS. If you didn't wish to fund me, why did you call me back?

ISABELLA. And just who authorized you to take this unilateral action?

FERDINAND. I don't need any stinking authorization, I'm an absolute monarch.

ISABELLA. Need I remind you that we have joined our two kingdoms by marriage, and you are NOT my sovereign, we rule jointly, my love, and this was MY project.

COLUMBUS. It was MY project.

FERDINAND. Your commission found him insane, so I simply sent word to him, to end his suspense, so as not to prolong his suffering, as a purely humanitarian gesture, and I didn't bother you about it because you and your demented confessor, the most holy Grand Inquisitor Torquemada, were busy displacing hundreds of thousands of innocent people from their homes and confiscating their possessions.

ISABELLA. I didn't hear any objections from you.

FERDINAND. I was busy running the country.

ISABELLA. And just how would you like to run your piddly little Aragon without the benefit of its union with my glorious Castile?

FERDINAND. Your glorious Castile is a dreary patch of scrub desert I wouldn't stop to take a leak in.

ISABELLA. Then why did you marry me to get it?

FERDINAND. Because I wanted to drive the Moors out of Spain. Certainly not because I wanted to bed down with the likes of YOU.

COLUMBUS. Excuse me—

ISABELLA. You seem to enjoy it well enough, when you can get yourself up for it.

JUANA. Uh oh.

FERDINAND. Just what kind of a crack is that?

ISABELLA. It is not seemly for sovereigns to quarrel in the presence of commoners.

FERDINAND. Fine. You—Columbine. Get out.

COLUMBUS. But I was called back.

FERDINAND. Not by me you weren't. OUT.

ISABELLA. Stay right where you are. He was called back by ME. I believe that is my right. Or does the King wish to spend the rest of his natural life sleeping with his sheep dog?

(FERDINAND starts to retort, then thinks again.)

ISABELLA. Christopher, my dear friend, I've been discussing your case with my privy councillors, and it's been pointed out to me that financing your expedition would cost no more than, say, entertaining a visiting head of state. And considering the benefits to Spain if you should happen to get lucky, I've decided that a small amount of money may be found to finance your voyage. Unless of course the King my husband has any objections.

FERDINAND. YOUR money, I hope.

ISABELLA. We'll negotiate that at a later time.

FERDINAND. I knew it.

COLUMBUS. I'm deeply grateful to your majesties, but I have certain additional demands on which I cannot in good conscience compromise.

FERDINAND. Demands? You have demands?

COLUMBUS. I must be known henceforth and forever more as the Admiral of the Ocean Sea. I must be Governor of any and all islands I may discover.

FERDINAND. The man's an egomaniac.

COLUMBUS. I must have ten percent of all gold, gems or spices obtained on these voyages—

FERDINAND. Also an extortionist.

COLUMBUS. And these offices and emoluments must obtain for myself and my heirs to the end of time.

FERDINAND. He's demented. His mind is a fruit farm.

COLUMBUS. I'll need a fleet of ships, experienced crews—

ISABELLA. We can confiscate a couple of ships. The crews you'll have to find on your own. Is that a problem?

COLUMBUS. No. No problem. Thank you, your majesties, I promise you'll never regret this.

FERDINAND. I regret it already.

TORQUEMADA. And so you got your ships.

COLUMBUS. Yes, and there was no sin about it. It was all done for the greater glory of God.

TORQUEMADA. Perhaps. But we haven't heard from the prosecution yet.

COLUMBUS. I thought you were the prosecution.

TORQUEMADA. No, I'm the adjudicator, I'm absolutely impartial. The prosecution will present its case shortly.

COLUMBUS. But who would accuse me? What could I possibly be guilty of?

TORQUEMADA. I think you know.

(Above, a DARK FIGURE in a monk's habit and cowl appears on the shipwreck. COLUMBUS looks up at him. WIND blows in the tattered sails. LIGHTS fade and go out. The wind. End of Act I.)

ACT II

21 (The Tavern at Palos)

As the MUSIC plays, LIGHTS up on a tavern in Palos as the PEOPLE return to form the scene, wandering on from various directions, RODRIGO and the ANCIENT MARINER to drink together at the DR table with the PIG WOMAN, who is helping her pig to drink, and the CROCODILE GIRL, whose hand puppet is drunk. The CROW WOMAN serves them. At the other table DL are PINZON and ESTRELLA, with MARIA serving them. JUANA and FELIPA watch together eating popcorn in the crow's nest, TORQUEMADA from UR. DIRTY CARLOS, the bartender, is flirting with DESDEMONA L as COLUMBUS and DIEGO enter the tavern from UR. The BEGGAR trying to bum a drink off Dirty Carlos. Dark atmosphere.

COLUMBUS. (*To Dirty Carlos as HE crosses with bottles.*) Pardon me, I'm looking for a man named Pinzon.

(DIRTY CARLOS stops, looks at them, spits at Diego's feet and goes.)

DIEGO. Nice place. Great atmosphere. Can we go home now?
COLUMBUS. Don't show fear. (*To Desdemona.*) Excuse me, miss, I'm looking for a man named Pinzon.

75

(SHE *holds out her hand. COLUMBUS gives her some*
   money, which SHE puts in her bosom.)

DESDEMONA. Thanks. (*SHE spits at Diego's feet and*
walks over to join Estrella.)
DIEGO. Why do they spit on ME? Why don't they spit
on YOU? It was your idea.
COLUMBUS. (*Holding out money to the BEGGAR,*
who reaches for it. COLUMBUS pulls it back.) Pinzon.
Where is Pinzon?
BEGGAR. Gawwwww. Zzzabbbb. GAAA.

(HE *indicates Pinzon DL, a large, sullen, bearlike man at*
   the DL table. COLUMBUS gives the money to the
   BEGGAR, who then spits at Diego's feet.)

COLUMBUS. (*Crossing down to Pinzon, DIEGO*
trailing.) You're Pinzon?
PINZON. Not me.

(HE *is rubbing Estrella's bare legs, which are in his lap,*
   while DESDEMONA fusses with his hair behind him.)

COLUMBUS. That man said you were.
PINZON. That man has intercourse with farm animals.
Who the hell are you?
COLUMBUS. I'm the man who's going to make you a
legend.
PINZON. In this place I'm already a legend.

COLUMBUS. I'm going to make you a legend everywhere, and forever.

PINZON. And how are you going to do that? Are you going to teach me to fart through my nose?

(ESTRELLA and DESDEMONA laugh. HE drinks.)

COLUMBUS. I'm going to sail west over the ocean sea to China, and I'm going to take you with me.

PINZON. Why? What would that get me?

COLUMBUS. Besides the opportunity to extend the circumference of your legend beyond the wharfs and brothels of Palos, you'd also get a share of the spoils.

PINZON. As much as you?

COLUMBUS. No. You'd be one of the captains. I'm the Admiral.

PINZON. You are a pukebrained jackass.

COLUMBUS. Be careful, sir. I am not in the habit of allowing people to speak to me that way.

PINZON. You'll allow me.

COLUMBUS. If you think I'm afraid of you, you're mistaken.

PINZON. You're too stupid to be afraid of me. You need me. Everybody in Palos knows who you are. And nobody is interested.

COLUMBUS. All right. There are plenty of good sailors in the world.

PINZON. Too bad you're not one of them.

COLUMBUS. You're the best captain in Palos. I need a crew, and all the King will supply is a medley of petty thieves and sex offenders from his dungeons. I need real sailors, but nobody here will trust an Italian. You, they trust. If you sign up, I can get a crew.

PINZON. Now we've established why you need me. We've yet to establish why I need you.

COLUMBUS. Because without me you're going nowhere. With me, you can sail to China.

PINZON. You couldn't sail your finger up a chicken's ass.

COLUMBUS. I'm trying to give you the chance to become tremendously wealthy and you sit there belching up stupid vulgarities.

PINZON. If I can become wealthy by sailing to China, why do I need you?

COLUMBUS. Because I know how to get there, and what to do when I get there, and I have a commission from the King and Queen.

PINZON. Have you ever commanded a ship? Any ship?

COLUMBUS. I've spent the last twenty years of my life preparing to do this. I've been ignored, ridiculed, humiliated, patronized by the brain-dead, I've gone hungry, I've sat and listened to pompous lectures by academic morons about why this is impossible, and yet I'm here, and I've got my commission, and I'm going to do this, and you are going to come with me.

PINZON. (*Looking at him for a moment.*) I just had the most horrible feeling.

ESTRELLA I told you not to eat pork here.

PINZON. No, I just had this terrible premonition that I'm going to do exactly what this madman wants me to.

DESDEMONA. All people who sail on the water are insane. I want to die with the earth flat under my back.

PINZON. I think there's an excellent chance of that.

ESTRELLA You're not going with him, are you?

PINZON. How could I pass up this golden opportunity to sail off the edge of the world with a lunatic? It's the self-destructive man's dream voyage. (*HE stands up and puts the bottle down on the table, wobbles a bit, then straightens out.*) Come on, you imbecile. Let's get you some real sailors.

JUANA. (*Whistling and applauding from the crow's nest with Felipa.*) Yayyy, Christopher! Way to go, baby! Go fight win!

(*THEY wave at him. HE waves back.*)

22 (The Muster)

COLUMBUS and PINZON examining a line of sailors— the BEGGAR, DIRTY CARLOS, RODRIGO, the ANCIENT MARINER, DIEGO and the PIG WOMAN. Not a very impressive group. The GIRLS sit around and make fun of them.

PINZON. (*Glaring at this motley line of people.*) My God, what a collection of human waste.

ANCIENT MARINER. You ain't exactly the Queen of Sheba yourself.

ESTRELLA Hey, Pinzon, can I go? I'm good with sailors.

RODRIGO. Not really.

(ESTRELLA hits him.)

PINZON. No women. Women are bad luck.

DESDEMONA. (*Pointing to Columbus.*) HE is bad luck.

COLUMBUS. (*Indicating Dirty Carlos.*) What about that one? He looks strong.

PINZON. No. Troublemaker. The little wirey ones are better, and they last longer. Rodrigo, you want to come sail with me?

RODRIGO. I don't know, Captain. I think this Italian guy is crazy.

PINZON. Okay. More Chinese women for me, then. You ever see a Chinese woman, Rodrigo? Chinese women have milky white breasts, and they sing like angels when you make love to them, and they never get tired of you. Shame you're going to miss them. The breasts of Chinese women are something to see, and even more, to touch, and oh, to kiss with one's lips. Well, too bad for you. Maybe we'll take this fellow instead.

BEGGAR. Big gazookas? Haffa taka bath?

RODRIGO. Do these Chinese women like little fellas?

PINZON. That's what I hear.

RODRIGO. Okay, what the hell. Sign me up.

COLUMBUS. (*Taking Pinzon aside.*) You've never seen a Chinese woman in your life.

PINZON. So? Neither has he.

COLUMBUS. But isn't he going to be mad as hell if they turn out to be mean and ugly?

PINZON. Do you want me to tell him the truth, that you don't know your butt from a turnip? He knows that, he just wanted me to coax him a little, it gives him a bit of dignity. He'll spend most of the voyage thinking about Chinese women and it'll keep him from being too disturbed that he's probably going to end up in a shark's intestines. I hear you're good with women, Mr. Italian, but I think you're not so good with sailors. This does not bode well.

TORQUEMADA. And so you assembled your wretched crews from the refuse of Europe.

COLUMBUS. They were good crews and brave men. And we sailed in three small but quite adequate although somewhat leaky ships, out into the vast ocean sea.

TORQUEMADA. And were immediately lost.

COLUMBUS. I was never lost. I was just sailing in uncharted waters.

(Sound of GULLS.)

23 (The First Voyage)

Up on the ship, outward bound, COLUMBUS and PINZON staring out at the horizon. The BEGGAR, DIEGO, the ANCIENT MARINER. RODRIGO is up in the crow's nest. The downstage area is in eerie BLUE DARKNESS. Very lonely up there.

PINZON. You're lost.

COLUMBUS. There's land over there. I can smell it.

PINZON. That's me you smell. And I smell better than you.

COLUMBUS. The birds are all flying in that direction.

PINZON. They're getting the hell away from us because of the smell. And you've been fiddling with the records to make it seem like we haven't sailed as far as we have.

COLUMBUS. Do you accuse me of lying?

PINZON. I don't mind lying. I accuse you of stupidity.

COLUMBUS. If we don't find land tomorrow, we'll turn back.

PINZON. That's what you said yesterday.

COLUMBUS. But today I mean it.

PINZON. You said you meant it yesterday.

COLUMBUS. I don't care what I said yesterday.

PINZON. I know you don't. You're insane.

COLUMBUS. If you think I'm insane then why did you come?

PINZON. To protect the sailors from your incompetence. And perhaps because I'd like a bit of glory before my liver stops functioning altogether, and glory always seems to hover about the soft heads of people like you. Of course, so do flies.

COLUMBUS. This is my voyage and my glory. Don't forget that. I am not good at sharing.

PINZON. We're like two old nuns arguing over who's getting the highest bunk in heaven, when in fact both are going to hell.

(The ANCIENT MARINER approaches them.)

PINZON. Oh, God, here comes old barnacle brain again. Why on earth did you bring him along?

COLUMBUS. He's the only one who's been this way before. Tell me, old man, are we near land? Do you think we're nearing land?

ANCIENT MARINER. *(Looking out.)* There are three types of people: the living, the dead, and the sailors. The living are alive, the dead are dead, but the sailors are caught between, death all around, the deep ready to swallow them, one mis-step and they disappear forever beneath the cold water into fathomless darkness. And them that wait on shore can't know at any given time if the loved one's live or dead. They might be going about their daily tasks, imagining the beloved on his ship at sea, when all the while he's been rotting on the ocean floor, eyes picked out by crabs. Or they might have given him up for dead, then one day see him walking down the path to the house, shipwrecked young, returning old, with nothing in between but separation. A sailor's suspended like a dream between the light above and the dark below, he sails on unknown seas to an unknown destination, like everybody else, but for him the thing is simpler, is seen in its essential elements. The way to get there is to set out and go, you'll eventually get someplace or other, probably not where you were aiming at, but there you are, the alternative is to go nowhere. I'm going to break wind like an old Scotch bagpipe.

PINZON. That's it. I'm jumping overboard.

RODRIGO. LAND. LAND HO. LAND HO. LAND. LAND.

COLUMBUS. LAND? IS IT LAND? DO YOU SEE
LAND?

RODRIGO. NO, I'M JUST KIDDING, WHAT DO
YOU THINK, BEANHEAD? YES, DAMMIT. IT'S
LAND. LAND. IT'S LAND.

(Jubilation among the CREW.)

COLUMBUS. YOU SEE? DO YOU SEE? AM I
CRAZY NOW? AM I? HAH? *(HE is jumping up and
down, standing on his head, acting very crazy indeed.)* AM
I? HAH? AM I CRAZY? HAH? HA HAHHHHHHH? AM
I CRAZY? AM I? HA? HAH HAHHH?

24 (A Small Allegation)

TORQUEMADA watches him grimly.

JUANA. Calm down, Christopher. Try to pretend
you're normal.

COLUMBUS. But I want to tell you about the landing
on the island, our landfall was glorious, it was
magnificent, a moment in history which—

TORQUEMADA. I don't care. It's irrelevant.

COLUMBUS. It's not irrelevant, it's the summit of my
life. I did it. I sailed across the ocean to the west and made
landfall on the easternmost island of China—

TORQUEMADA. We have an allegation in relation to
this.

COLUMBUS. What allegation? I'm trying to tell you that we found land, we walked through the water and onto the land, and—

RODRIGO. I saw the land.

COLUMBUS. Yes, yes, we all saw it—

RODRIGO. I saw it first.

COLUMBUS. What difference does it make who saw it first? The important thing is that—

RODRIGO. You told us the first man to see land would get a pension for life from the Queen. You promised us that. And what did I get?

COLUMBUS. I don't know what you got. What did you get?

RODRIGO. Nothing. Not a cent. I got nothing.

COLUMBUS. This is something you should take up with the Spanish government, not me.

RODRIGO. It was you who took my money, you charlatan, you filthy pompous liar, you told the King and Queen it was you who saw land first, you made up a story about having seen a light from the west earlier in the evening—

COLUMBUS. I did see it, I just kept it to myself.

RODRIGO. Fine, then I saw it before that, and also kept it to myself. I saw it before I left Spain and kept it to myself.

COLUMBUS. I didn't want to give the men false hope.

RODRIGO. You spent the whole voyage giving us false hope, when you weren't in your cabin sleeping in your featherbed while I froze to death in the crow's nest. I saw land, and shouted out when I saw it, and you took my reward and used it to give a pension to your whore. (*HE points to BEATRIZ, who watches from the bed.*) You're a thief and a liar and a hypocrite, and you should burn in hell for it.

COLUMBUS. I'm sorry, I didn't know. I didn't realize. But this is trivial, it's a trivial incident.

RODRIGO. NOT TO ME IT ISN'T. IT WAS MY WHOLE LIFE.

COLUMBUS. Let me tell you what happened once we stepped onto the land. Let me remind you what's really important here—

25   (Savages)

A VOICE from up on the ship structure.

PROSECUTOR. I can tell you what happened then.

COLUMBUS. (*Looking up and seeing the dark figure in the monk's habit and cowl on the shipwreck.*) What do you know about it?

PROSECUTOR. I was there. Don't you recognize me?

COLUMBUS. I can't see your face.

(The PROSECUTOR lowers the cowl. He is an Indian.)

COLUMBUS. You're one of the savages?

PROSECUTOR. Yes. I'm one of the savages. I saw you step off your little boat and claim our island and all the land as far as you could see for the King and Queen of Spain.

COLUMBUS. That's what I was sent to do. I don't remember seeing you in particular there.

(The three NATIVE GIRLS have appeared DR and look shyly at the sailors. RODRIGO, DIEGO, the ANCIENT MARINER, the BEGGAR and PINZON approach cautiously and begin to interact with them.)

PROSECUTOR. And what did you think of these savages you'd found?

COLUMBUS. They were beautiful people, mostly very young. I remember the women most clearly for some reason, they were more or less naked, but painted various colors.

PROSECUTOR. How did they behave? What were they like?

COLUMBUS. They were gentle, friendly, completely unashamed of their state of undress, charming. I got down on my knees there on the shore and thanked God for allowing me to discover such lovely people. It was like the garden of Eden.

PROSECUTOR. Really? And who was the snake?

COLUMBUS. I beg your pardon?

JUANA. Yeah. I didn't like the tone of that. I object.

TORQUEMADA. You be quiet. You've had your chance. Now it's his turn.

PROSECUTOR. And what did you turn to your friend Diego and say?

COLUMBUS. How can I remember exactly what I said? Why are you asking me these stupid questions?

PROSECUTOR. (*Pointing to Diego.*) You. What did he say?

DIEGO. Just that we must bring a few of these beautiful people home to show the Queen.

PROSECUTOR. And?

DIEGO. And he thanked God that he'd been blessed to discover an entire race of what he hoped would become an excellent and abundant supply of slaves.

PROSECUTOR. Slaves.

COLUMBUS. Well, servants. These people were innocent savages. One had to think of their immortal souls. As sla—servants they could be made into Christians and saved. Surely there was no sin in that. They were like children, they would share anything with us, they were happy to show us around the island, they loved the trinkets we gave them.

(The native GIRLS are giggling and pointing at the sailors. RODRIGO does tricks for them. THEY pull the Ancient Mariner's beard, etc.)

PROSECUTOR. (*To the Native Girls.*) And what did you think of the strangers? It's all right, you can tell us.

FIRST NATIVE GIRL. At first we thought they might be gods, and we were a little afraid of them, but the first thing they did when they got onshore was relieve themselves, and when we saw their instruments for making water, we knew they could not be gods.

SECOND NATIVE GIRL. Also, they smelled awful, and they didn't speak any civilized language, they made these ridiculous noises like dogs barking.

THIRD NATIVE GIRL. And they had the most idiotic fascination for our jewelry. They wore horribly smelly skins and rags over their bodies, which were white like maggots and hairy like pigs, and all they could think about was our little yellow stones.

PROSECUTOR. You mean the gold.

(PINZON is examining the gold jewelry.)

FIRST NATIVE GIRL. Yes, that's what they called it. They kept demanding to know where we got them, so we told them, a much bigger island, which they insisted on pronouncing wrong—

SECOND NATIVE GIRL. Cuba.

COLUMBUS. China?

THIRD NATIVE GIRL. Cuba

COLUMBUS. China. She's saying China. I knew it.

(PINZON slips away quietly up left.)

FIRST NATIVE GIRL. They were very stupid people. We took them wherever they wanted to go, showed them lovely islands with many trees but they were desperate to see a person they called the Emperor of China, so we took them to meet my grandfather, who is very old and has no teeth, but they were disappointed. They seemed to carry sadness around with them like a disease. And they couldn't get along with each other.

26 (Shipwreck)

COLUMBUS. Pinzon? What happened to Pinzon? Where's the *Pinta*?

DIEGO. He's gone.

COLUMBUS. Gone where? I didn't order him to go anywhere.

DIEGO. The natives told him there's an island west of here where you can gather up gold on the beach by moonlight.

COLUMBUS. My God, what a waste of time. We're looking for the Emperor of China.

DIEGO. I don't think Pinzon cares about the Emperor of China.

COLUMBUS. That traitor. After all I did for him.

DIEGO. There's nothing we can do about it. He'll just say he got separated from us. We'd better gather up what gold we can and get back to Spain before he does.

TORQUEMADA. So you didn't find the Emperor of China?

COLUMBUS. No, but we found many pine trees.

PROSECUTOR. Which you immediately cut down.

COLUMBUS. We discovered the island of Hispaniola.

PROSECUTOR. Which you enslaved.

COLUMBUS. Which we colonized. And we found gold there.

PROSECUTOR. Which you stole.

COLUMBUS. The natives were more than happy to trade with us.

PROSECUTOR. For items that were worthless.

COLUMBUS. Not to them. Worth is a relative concept.

PROSECUTOR. And did this barter include their women?

COLUMBUS. They believed in sharing. And the women didn't mind. They were naked and happy.

PROSECUTOR. How could you tell? Did you ask them?

COLUMBUS. I could tell they were naked. They seemed happy.

PROSECUTOR. (*To the Native Girls.*) Were you happy?

SECOND NATIVE GIRL. At first it was all right. But later on I decided I didn't like them very much, because I realized they couldn't see me. I was invisible to them.

COLUMBUS. You weren't invisible, I saw you, and if you objected to anything we did, why didn't you say something?

SECOND NATIVE GIRL. I was given by one man who was red to another man who was white. My objections had nothing to do with it.

COLUMBUS. I fail to see what the minor complaints of one little savage girl could possibly have to do with the fate of my immortal soul. Why don't you ask about the glorious accomplishments of this voyage?

PROSECUTOR. Like losing your flagship?

COLUMBUS. That was unfortunate. We were having a Christmas party. The sea was calm. We left a boy on watch. And the *Santa Maria* drifted onto a reef and broke apart. We did salvage most of the cargo.

PROSECUTOR. How did you manage that?

COLUMBUS. The natives helped us bring it to shore.

PROSECUTOR. Where no doubt they stole it all.

COLUMBUS. No, they stood watch over it.

PROSECUTOR. You mean these pagans, who loved your precious trinkets so much, stood watch over them all night and stole nothing?

COLUMBUS. Apparently they had some sort of primitive sense of honor.

PROSECUTOR. But you'd soon take care of that, wouldn't you?

COLUMBUS. Of what exactly does this person accuse me? Why is he permitted to speak to me this way? It was these same natives who later butchered my men.

JUANA. Really? Why would they do that?

PROSECUTOR. Yes, tell us why, Admiral.

COLUMBUS. How should I know why? They were savages.

TORQUEMADA. The savages are not on trial at present. Just tell us what happened after the shipwreck.

COLUMBUS. With the lumber from the *Santa Maria* I built a fort and left Diego in charge. Then I sailed back to Spain. My voyage to China had been an enormous success.

27 (The Birds)

The JESTER blows a fanfare and the Spanish court appears again, amid a great horrible din of exotic BIRD SQUAWKING, really hideous, SHADOWS of birds

flying back and forth—this done with LIGHTS,
SOUND EFFECTS and actor NOISES—no real birds.

JUANA. (*Running to greet Columbus, jumping in his
arms again.*) Christopher! Did you bring me a present?

FERDINAND. What the hell is all that racket? And the
smell. Did something die in here?

COLUMBUS. It's the Chinese birds, your majesty.

FERDINAND. (*Deafened by the squawking.*) WHAT?

COLUMBUS. I have brought you these many-colored
birds from exotic China. I have returned from the Orient
with a multitude of wonders for you.

FERDINAND. How much gold did you bring?

COLUMBUS. WHAT?

FERDINAND. Gold. How much gold?

COLUMBUS. Some gold, and the promise of much
more.

FERDINAND. But how much did you bring me NOW?

COLUMBUS. Much less than I will bring home on my
next voyage. But look at these birds. Look at their many
bright colors. Listen to their various and lovely songs.

FERDINAND. Just what do you expect me to do with
all these goddamned birds?

ISABELLA. Your birds are very beautiful, Admiral.
We're happy to accept them. What else have you brought?

COLUMBUS. (*Clapping his hands twice.*) Bring in the
gifts.

(*The ANCIENT MARINER leads in the three NATIVE
GIRLS by ropes which attach to collars around their
necks. Each has a muzzle on her mouth.*)

COLUMBUS. I bring you these slaves from the Orient. I've put muzzles on them as a precautionary measure, as one or two of the sailors was bitten by them on the return voyage, but you needn't worry, they are by nature simple and gentle, and will make good Christians and excellent slaves.

ISABELLA. That's very impressive, Admiral, but my husband and I need gold to run our kingdom.

COLUMBUS. That's why I've got to go back as soon as possible, this time with a great fleet of ships, to bring you the real treasures of China.

ISABELLA. I think that's a fair request, don't you, darling? He has, after all, done exactly what he said he would.

FERDINAND. He's found some islands and brought back birds, a few savages and a piddling amount of gold. I see no proof he got anywhere near China. But clearly there is something out there. All right. You'll get your fleet of ships. But if you don't return with substantial amounts of gold, no more ships, no more voyages, no more Admiral, is that clear?

COLUMBUS. Yes, your majesty. Thank you, your majesty.

FERDINAND. And don't bring me any more of these frigging birds.

ISABELLA. Oh, they're not so bad. Look how beautiful that big one is.

(A loud SQUAWK. FERDINAND looks up and a large bomb of white glop falls in his face—do this with a

crowd look and vocalization high to low to indicate the falling, with the King reacting at the climax by slapping to his face a hand in which he has preset concealed white glop. The KING stomps furiously over to get a gun from Bobadilla, shoots up into the air—use dummy gun and sound effect from wings—no blanks— and BIRDS fall everywhere. The ANCIENT MARINER gets the NATIVE GIRLS to run and retrieve the birds.)

PROSECUTOR. So you took these innocent people across the ocean to the court of Spain, put muzzles and collars on them and led them around like dogs, people who thought they were making a small voyage to another island, who had no idea what was happening to them.

COLUMBUS. They came of their own free will. They couldn't have survived in Spain without somebody to protect them. Who better than the King and Queen? Where would they live better than at the palace? Right?

(HE looks to Juana for support, but SHE hesitates, horrified by the muzzles.)

COLUMBUS. I don't see what all this fuss is about, over a few Chinese women. I had done a great thing. I found the western route to China. Does that not justify a few small oversights? Were they not little more than slaves to their chieftains on the islands we took them from? Right?

(HE looks at Juana. SHE looks at him, and then begins removing the muzzles from the Native Girls.)

PROSECUTOR. And did you have no doubts? Did you never once stop to think about the consequences of what you were doing?

COLUMBUS. Great men do not have doubts.

28 (Doubts)

COLUMBUS sits with BEATRIZ, having doubts.

BEATRIZ. What are you thinking about? Hello? Christopher? Ahoy? (*HE is lost in thought. Finally SHE screams in his ear.*) AAAAAAHHHHHHHHHH.

COLUMBUS. (*Falling over, holding his ears.*) What? What is it?

BEATRIZ. I was just making sure you weren't dead. Talk to me. I haven't seen you in months. What are you thinking about?

COLUMBUS. They can't have souls.

BEATRIZ. Who? The King and Queen?

COLUMBUS. The natives we brought back. They can't have souls.

BEATRIZ. Why can't they? They're people just like us.

COLUMBUS. Because they're not Christians, they can't be Christians because they know nothing of Christianity, therefore, if they had souls, they'd be damned to hell, so they can't have souls, because God would not be that cruel.

BEATRIZ. Of course he would. Read the Bible. God can smite people for just pissing against a wall. He can do anything he wants to. He made me fall desperately in love with a lunatic. What greater proof of his cruelty do you want?

COLUMBUS. Blasphemy is not attractive in a woman. (*HE looks at her.*) Let's go to bed.

BEATRIZ. Wait a minute, listen, they ARE people like us, Christopher. If we have souls, so do they. You mustn't think of them as not human. That is not a Christian thing.

COLUMBUS. Then it's our duty to make them Christians and save their souls.

BEATRIZ. Maybe you don't need to save their souls. Maybe God's not such a religious fanatic as you think. Maybe I'm wrong about his cruelty. Maybe there are as many paths to salvation as there are to hell. Maybe your job is simply to treat them decently and respect them as human beings and let them take care of their own souls.

COLUMBUS. I am now going to make desperate, violent love to every part of your anatomy.

(HE goes after her but SHE eludes him.)

BEATRIZ. First tell me why you left Diego on the other side of the ocean.

COLUMBUS. I needed somebody I could trust in charge of the garrison. He volunteered to stay. He'll be fine, the natives are friendly.

BEATRIZ. But will they still be friendly when they realize you came there to take their land and make them slaves?

COLUMBUS. First you're telling me they're people like us, and then you're worried they're going to murder Diego.

BEATRIZ. It's because they're people like us that I'm worried. You talked him into going with you, you probably also talked him into staying. You shouldn't have left him there, especially not in charge. He's not good at telling people what to do. If anything happens to him—

COLUMBUS. Nothing's going to happen to him, I promise.

BEATRIZ. All right, but I mean it. If anything happens to him, I'll never forgive you. Never.

(COLUMBUS looks at her, uneasy.)

29 (Butchers)

TORQUEMADA. We are not impressed by your harlot's pathetic attempts to reinvent Christian dogma. We must make a note to look into her orthodoxy at a later date.

COLUMBUS. Leave her alone. She's the finest person I ever knew.

TORQUEMADA. If the finest person you knew was a blasphemous whore, you didn't keep very good company, did you?

COLUMBUS. Neither did Christ. And she's not a whore, she was loyal to me all those years.

PROSECUTOR. And were you loyal to her?

COLUMBUS. Mostly.

TORQUEMADA. To speak of loyalty in connection with whores and to imply some sort of virtue in this is absurd. Now, you made your second voyage—

COLUMBUS. Which was a tremendous success.

PROSECUTOR. You lost the entire fleet.

COLUMBUS. I didn't lose them, they sank. And some turned back.

PROSECUTOR. And what happened to your friend Diego, who had taken you into his home, introduced you to his cousin Beatriz, sailed with you on your voyage, and stayed behind at your bidding?

COLUMBUS. You know what happened to him. You savages butchered him.

PROSECUTOR. Your men were drunk all the time, they took our women, and when we protested they beat and humiliated us. They were guests in our land and they behaved worse than animals.

COLUMBUS. It was not your land, I claimed it for the King and Queen of Spain.

PROSECUTOR. You stole it for them.

COLUMBUS. (*To Torquemada.*) Are you going to let this pagan insult me like this? This butcher who slaughtered my friend Diego and all his men? Diego never hurt a soul in his life.

PROSECUTOR. While your good-natured friend Diego sat drinking and joking, your men burned our villages, raped our women, stole our food, cut down every tree on the island, dug up our crops looking for gold—

COLUMBUS. I ordered them not to harm anyone.

PROSECUTOR. That's like ordering your horse not to shit.

TORQUEMADA. What concerns me here is why you did not do more to turn these savages into Christians?

COLUMBUS. We tried to convert them.

PROSECUTOR. You told us about a kind and loving God and then you made us into slaves and slaughtered us. You were the savages. For what you did to us alone you deserve to burn in agony in the flames of your Christian hell run by your forgiving Christian god forever.

TORQUEMADA. I will decide who goes to hell, thank you.

COLUMBUS. I was good to you. When a chief and his wife and beautiful daughters, all naked as Eve in the garden, wanted to sail to Spain to greet the Queen, I might have brought them, they were an impressive sight, but I took pity on them, made excuses and sent them home. Was that the act of a savage?

PROSECUTOR. You save six on a whim to soothe your conscience and then butcher six million.

COLUMBUS. I never butchered anybody.

TORQUEMADA. You both miss the point. You should have brought this chief and his family to Spain, where their souls might have been saved. But you sent them off in their pagan nakedness and in so doing damned them to the flames of hell for all eternity. Was that a Christian action?

COLUMBUS. So I'm damned if I do and damned if I don't. I was trying to do right. You must look at the bigger picture—

PROSECUTOR. Yes, let's do that. When this man arrived on the island of Hispaniola there were two hundred fifty thousand native inhabitants. A few years later there were less than five hundred. This butcher destroyed a whole race of people. You should write about this man in your history books with the foulest monsters who ever lived. The suffering, injustice and destruction this man has caused are beyond calculation. Shame on him, and shame on anyone stupid enough to blindly worship him.

COLUMBUS. I never meant to harm anyone.

PROSECUTOR. You saw what was happening and did nothing.

COLUMBUS. We were three Italians in a nest of Spanish sailors. They were greedy and ignorant and wouldn't listen to us. What could I have done? If I'd tried to stop them, my men would have killed me. It was not my job to die for a bunch of cannibals.

PROSECUTOR. Didn't your God die for the sake even of those who killed him? And as for cannibals, tell us, why don't you, what happened on the return to Spain after your disastrous second voyage?

(Sound of GULLS.)

30 (Cannibals)

On the ship, COLUMBUS writes in his log. The NATIVE GIRLS and the ANCIENT MARINER visible in the bow area. FRANCISCO approaches Columbus.

FRANCISCO. Sir?
COLUMBUS. Yes? What is it?

FRANCISCO. The men are tired of the tiny rations, sir.

COLUMBUS. So am I, but it can't be helped, we're becalmed, we don't know how long it's going to be until we get a decent tail wind, we've got to ration food.

FRANCISCO. Sir, the crew has a suggestion about that. The crew thought, sir, that the large number of natives on board is what's made the rations so small.

COLUMBUS. They've got to eat, too. A dead slave's no good to anybody, is he?

FRANCISCO. Neither's a dead sailor, sir. And some of the crew, sir, was wanting to perhaps help economize the rations by throwing a few of the natives overboard.

COLUMBUS. I don't think that's a good idea.

FRANCISCO. Oh, me neither, sir. I talked them out of it. My idea, sir, is that we should eat them.

COLUMBUS. Eat them?

FRANCISCO. Yes sir. Some of them is cannibals themselves, sir. It would serve them right. I'm a good cook, sir, I could make a number of very tasty dishes out of them—the meat's much like pork, sir. So I hear.

(Pause.)

COLUMBUS. I'll think about it.

PROSECUTOR. And you call US savages.

COLUMBUS. Nobody was eaten on my ship. Not to my knowledge.

PROSECUTOR. But you didn't forbid it. You considered it.

COLUMBUS. I pretended to consider it. If I'd made a big issue of it, I might have caused a mutiny.

PROSECUTOR. You were the cannibals. You devoured us. There was nothing left of us when you were through. We became ghosts.

TORQUEMADA. So you returned from your second voyage in disgrace, having lost nearly everything. You were so ashamed you didn't even see the King and Queen, you went straight to your whore instead.

COLUMBUS. There was something I had to tell her.

31 (Beatriz Grieving)

BEATRIZ. You killed him. You murdered Diego.

COLUMBUS. The natives killed him. I'm sorry.

BEATRIZ. You swore nothing would happen to him. You promised.

COLUMBUS. I should not have promised.

BEATRIZ. Get out.

COLUMBUS. Don't send me away. I've had a terrible voyage. I've lost everything. The King and Queen won't see me.

BEATRIZ. Why don't you visit the Governess of Gomera?

COLUMBUS. I don't know what you mean.

BEATRIZ. On both your voyages out, you stopped at the island of Gomera—

COLUMBUS. To get provisions.

BEATRIZ. Where a very beautiful widow governs the island for the Spanish monarchy—

COLUMBUS. I know this woman, and I presented my respects to her—

BEATRIZ. Your respects weren't all you presented to her.

COLUMBUS. Who told you this?

BEATRIZ. It's no secret. Everybody knows about it.

COLUMBUS. Nothing happened.

BEATRIZ. How can you stand there and lie to me?

COLUMBUS. I promise you—

BEATRIZ. I've had enough of your promises. I've seen you lie, I know when you're lying.

COLUMBUS. If I lie it's only to spare you more grief. If you want the truth, all right, the truth is, I slept with this woman on each of my voyages out. For all I knew, I was never coming back. You know I've never been able to resist a beautiful woman. You know how I am.

BEATRIZ. Yes, I know how you are.

COLUMBUS. I need you.

BEATRIZ. Then prove it. Give up these moronic voyages and stay here with me and your children. Make maps. Will you?

COLUMBUS. I've not yet actually heard from the King and Queen. It may still be possible that—

BEATRIZ. You want me to forgive you but you always go away and leave me and betray me and lie to me—

COLUMBUS. I betrayed you with one woman on two occasions when I was going out to sail off the edge of the world. If the King and Queen want me back, I must go back, I'm the Admiral of the Ocean Sea.

BEATRIZ. You're the stupidest man God ever made. I can't imagine how you've escaped ending up at the bottom of the ocean. Maybe on your next trip you should explore the ocean floor, you can claim it for the King and Queen, and kill all the fish.

COLUMBUS. You know you love me and you're going to forgive me sooner or later, so why prolong the agony for both of us?

BEATRIZ. No, this is the end. I don't want to see you any more. You will send money each month to provide for your children, and when they're old enough I'll send them to you, and then you'll owe me nothing more, but I don't ever want to see your face again, is that clear?

COLUMBUS. It makes no sense—

BEATRIZ. Then you should understand it perfectly, because in your whole life you've never for one moment made any sense at all.

COLUMBUS. You don't mean this, you'll forgive me, I'm a man who's impossible not to forgive, you said that yourself.

BEATRIZ. It's not a question of forgiveness, but of self-preservation and perhaps self-respect. I forgive you. I just don't want to see you any more. Goodbye. (*SHE starts away.*)

COLUMBUS. Wait. Please. All right. You're right. (*SHE hesitates.*) I've been proud and selfish. I've let my obsessions control my life. I'll forget about the sea. I'll put on a monk's habit, I'll abandon this pride that's caused God to abandon me, and you to abandon me. I'll live in a monastery. Perhaps in time I'll be worthy of you again.

BEATRIZ. You're posturing.

COLUMBUS. I mean it, I swear.

BEATRIZ. You've sworn before.

COLUMBUS. Not this I haven't. I'll give it all up. I'll live in a monastery for a year, to prove to you I'm serious. You know this is the greatest sacrifice a man like me could make. At the end of the year, if you'll have me, I'll ask you to marry me. And if you refuse, I'll live as a monk forever.

BEATRIZ. You're acting out a fantasy.

COLUMBUS. Will you just give me a chance? Please? You're all I have left. If I lose you, I have nothing.

(THEY look at each other for a long moment. BEATRIZ is just about to speak when FELIPA comes in, as the Maid.)

FELIPA. Excuse me, mum.

BEATRIZ. Not now.

FELIPA. But there's a man downstairs from the King and Queen, mum. He says they want to see the Admiral immediately.

(COLUMBUS looks at her, hesitates.)

BEATRIZ. (*Looking back at him sadly.*) Go on. You don't want to disappoint them, do you?

(HE hesitates. Then HE goes. BEATRIZ is left standing there alone.)

32 (Money)

The Spanish court. The JESTER starts to blow his horn.
The KING jumps on him and wrestles the horn away.
The JESTER pulls out a smaller horn and toots a
fanfare in the King's ear.

FERDINAND. (*Deciding to put off killing the Jester.*
To Columbus.) So. You promise gold and bring back very
little. You promise peaceful, civilized Chinese, and what
we get is a murderous insurrection of cannibal savages.
You promise trade with Asia and can't find anybody to
trade with. The Portuguese are making a fortune on the
Gold Coast while we make next to nothing and lose a
whole fleet. Your ships sink, your geography is fantasy,
your calculations are absurd, the slaves you bring back die,
and all you've discovered thus far is a quagmire that eats
my money.
    COLUMBUS. Your Majesty, look on the bright side. If
only—
    FERDINAND. Be quiet. I've already decided what I'm
going to do with you.
    COLUMBUS. Please, sir, if only you'd—
    ISABELLA. He's sending you back.
    COLUMBUS. Pardon?
    FERDINAND. I'm sending you back. Prince John has
been making noises about sailing west, and whatever the
hell it is you've found, I'll be damned if I'm going to give
it to the Portuguese, however worthless it may be. How
soon can you leave?

COLUMBUS. Oh, thank you, your Majesties—
ISABELLA. You're very welcome, Admiral.
JUANA. What about Beatriz?
COLUMBUS. Pardon?
JUANA. Beatriz. What about Beatriz?
COLUMBUS. She'll be all right. She understands. I'll send money.

(JUANA looks at him, then at Beatriz alone DR.)

PROSECUTOR. I think it might be instructive if you explained just how you financed this third voyage.
COLUMBUS. The money came from various sources.
PROSECUTOR. You sold human beings.
COLUMBUS. Certain of the surviving natives were sold to help finance my third voyage, yes, but, this was all for the greater glory of God, we were going to Christianize millions—
PROSECUTOR. Is this the God you worship? A God who is glorified by the enslavement of his creatures?
COLUMBUS. God works in mysterious ways. Why shouldn't I?
PROSECUTOR. And you were not at all troubled by this?
COLUMBUS. I was troubled, at this time, by a number of things, which is why I stopped, on the voyage out, at the island of Porto Santo, where I had spent the happiest years of my life with my wife Felipa, and walked again where I had walked with her as a young man.

(BIRD sounds, gentle.)

33 (Return to Porto Santo)

COLUMBUS walks on Porto Santo. FELIPA waits there, in white, beautiful, as before.

FELIPA. So you've come back to me. It's been a very long time, Christopher, even for a dead person to wait.

COLUMBUS. I'm sorry, I was occupied. But I kept seeing you—I mean, thinking I'd seen you, in the oddest places, in people who clearly were not you. It was so strange, like you were always there, only just out of my reach—just at the corner of my eye.

FELIPA. Things have gone very well for you.

COLUMBUS. No they haven't.

FELIPA. But you're famous, all the dead people say so.

COLUMBUS. I'm an object of ridicule. They call me the Admiral of the Mosquitoes. I'm laughed at all over Europe.

FELIPA. But the King and Queen thought enough of you to send you back again.

COLUMBUS. The King detests me. The Queen pities me. They do it for their own purposes. I am not what I had wished to be. I am not a great man.

FELIPA. And how does one get to be a great man, Christopher?

COLUMBUS. If I knew that, I'd be one.

FELIPA. You have a nice woman who loves you.

COLUMBUS. Beatriz hates me now.

FELIPA. I don't think so.

COLUMBUS. She won't see me. I don't blame her. I promised her I wouldn't sail again, but I couldn't keep my promise for five minutes. What am I doing wrong? Why do I feel like some sort of criminal?

FELIPA. You could forget about all that and stay here with me.

COLUMBUS. I can't. I'm not dead yet. I'm still afflicted with hope.

FELIPA. Then you'd better go and find whatever truth is waiting for you, out in the ocean sea. I don't think I can help you any more. I'm beginning to disappear. Even the dead eventually disappear. Death is like the ocean sea. Very wide and very deep. I'm very far away now. I'm almost gone.

(The LIGHT fades on her and goes out.)

34 (Mermaids)

TORQUEMADA. And did you stop again at the island of Gomera to visit your other whore, the Governess?

COLUMBUS. We stopped there merely to take on cheese and goats. Then we sailed south, towards the Equator, and were becalmed. It was so hot, we feared the ships would catch fire from the closeness of the sun. The barrel hoops broke and the wine and water spilled out. The goat meat went bad and began to stink. The goats stunk. The cheese stunk. The heat began to give us delusions. I thought hell must be like this, your flesh burns and peels off, and everything smells like cheese and goats. There were women on board, to colonize the islands, and they'd chatter among themselves at night, and in my troubled sleep I could hear mermaids.

FIRST MERMAID. Look at him, the Admiral of the Stinking Cheese.

SECOND MERMAID. He's too old for this.

THIRD MERMAID. He's sick. We should comfort him. We should let him touch our breasts.

FIRST MERMAID. No, I don't think so.

SECOND MERMAID. Perhaps he'd like to take a swim.

THIRD MERMAID. Would you like to join us in the water, Admiral? We could frolic together among the sharks, the giant squid—

FIRST MERMAID. The sharks love you.

SECOND MERMAID. That's why they follow the ship. They think you're a great man.

THIRD MERMAID. Wouldn't you like to make love to us under the water?

COLUMBUS. Why do you torment me?

FIRST MERMAID. Desire torments you. Eliminate desire and you will no longer be tormented.

COLUMBUS. I can't. Desire is who I am.

SECOND MERMAID. Then torment is who you are. Yourself am hell.

COLUMBUS. Can I just touch your breasts, just for a moment, can I just suck some nourishment from your breasts, please?

THIRD MERMAID. Your mouth is dry. You can't touch us. You're dying of loneliness. The water is cool. Beneath the ocean all is very cool. Come into the water.

FIRST MERMAID. Come into the water.

SECOND MERMAID. Christopher.

THIRD MERMAID. Come into the water.

COLUMBUS. I thought I was going mad. Perhaps I was. But at last we made landfall.

TORQUEMADA. And where did you imagine you were this time?

35 (Vespucci)

COLUMBUS. It was much further south than China could be, so I decided I'd discovered a new continent.

VESPUCCI. There he goes again. He think's Venezuela's just south of China. What a booby.

COLUMBUS. Who is that? Who is speaking?

VESPUCCI. He also decided this place must be the original Garden of Eden. The man's got holes in his bucket.

COLUMBUS. Don't you dare vomit insults at me. I see who you are now. This man stole from me. Someone took my journal and sailed to Margarita island, which I discovered, to search for pearls, a clear violation of my exclusive agreement with the Spanish sovereigns, and worst of all took with him this Florentine cretin Amerigo Vespalucci.

VESPUCCI. Vespucci.

COLUMBUS. This clown wrote a stupid account of his voyage, lied about the date to make it appear that he had discovered this place, and called it a NEW WORLD, and when some other idiot got hold of this malicious misinformation and put it on a map, it came to be known by the revolting name of America.

VESPUCCI. It sounds better than Christophornia.

COLUMBUS. I'll kill him. Let me kill him. (*H E begins chasing Vespucci all over the stage.*) That's what opened the gates. Then all of them began coming, every two-bit conquistador got in a boat and sailed into my territory to take slaves and pearls and gold. That's when the real horrors started, when my beautiful domain was infested with these piratical vermin—it was all his fault. I'll kill him.

VESPUCCI. Don't hurt me. I'm a great man.

COLUMBUS. You're a lying swine, and you stole my glory.

VESPUCCI. What can I say? I was in the right place at the right time. Why should they name a continent after YOU? You thought you'd discovered China.

COLUMBUS. I did discover China.

VESPUCCI. The Chinese discovered China. You discovered a terrible way to get there. China already had a perfectly good name. What I discovered did not. So they called it by my name. And, mark my words, one day there will be a great nation in the place you still insist on calling China, and they will call it, not by your name, but by mine, they will proudly call it THE UNITED STATES OF VESPUCCI.

COLUMBUS. (*Being restrained with some difficulty.*) I'LL KILL HIM. I'LL PULL HIS HEAD OFF.

VESPUCCI. You got everything wrong. You thought Venezuela was an island. You took possession in a formal ceremony attended by four dirty sailors and a thousand chattering monkeys, fit subjects for you.

COLUMBUS. You're the monkey. Usurper. Charlatan.

TORQUEMADA. (*As COLUMBUS chokes Vespucci.*) All right, that's enough, stop it, both of you.

VESPUCCI. He vilifies me, but all his life, even when he did accidentally discover something, he didn't know what the hell he'd discovered, he always thought it was something else. He spent his whole life pissing in the dark.

TORQUEMADA. SILENCE. I hate Italians, they have too many emotions. Emotions come from the Devil—which is why Dante found so many Italians in Hell. Now, we're going to finish this thing up, I've got some writers in the oven, so get on with it.

36 (Chains)

COLUMBUS. It was there, at the place called the Serpent's Mouth, that a great tidal wave nearly swallowed the ship. It sent us towering high in the air, so we could feel God's breath upon us, and then down so far we could see the bottom of the ocean, the corpses and whale skeletons and the ruins of ancient cities. We sailed through the dark into the mouth of the serpent, to a forest of undersea evil lurking beneath us, waiting to swallow me, and I began, for the first time in my life, to feel death close to me. But we made it safely to Hispaniola, where some opportunistic halfwit had joined with the natives and revolted against the garrison.

FRANCISCO. I will not give in. These are my demands. (*HE hands a piece of paper to Columbus.*)

COLUMBUS. (*Reading:*) Dearest Honeybucket, I long desperately for your throbbing loin-thing—

FRANCISCO. (*Snatching it back.*) Wait, no, sorry, that's a letter from my sister. My comrades the natives and I protest your oppressive policies. The gold tribute you demand is destroying their island. You send hundreds back to Europe as slaves and they die there—

COLUMBUS. On the last voyage you wanted to eat these people, and now all of a sudden you've become their champion?

FRANCISCO. I have recently become politically enlightened. And you treat your own men almost as badly. We come here, we risk our lives for you and we end up with nothing.

COLUMBUS. All right, look, I'm tired, stop the insurrection and I'll give every Spaniard a plot of his very own land, and all the natives who live on these plots will be safe from transportation to Europe—they will instead become the slaves of the colonist who owns the land. Is that fair?

FRANCISCO. Sounds fair to me. All right. I accept.

PROSECUTOR. Wait a minute. What about us? What about your native allies you've become so enlightened about?

FRANCISCO. Sorry. Business is business, and so is politics.

PROSECUTOR. Pigs. Demons. Liars. Hypocrites.

BOBADILLA. (*Coming in grandly, accompanied by a fanfare from the JESTER.*) Excuse me. There will be no deals made unless I make them. I'm in charge here.

COLUMBUS. You're not in charge. I'm in charge.

BOBADILLA. Not any more. I, Bobadilla, have just arrived from Spain, I'm in charge now, and I have papers to prove it.

COLUMBUS. My mandate is from the King and Queen.

BOBADILLA. So's mine, and it supersedes yours.

COLUMBUS. That's impossible. My mandate is forever.

BOBADILLA. If you resist me, I'll have to put you in chains.

COLUMBUS. Don't be a fool. No one here would dare put me in chains.

BOBADILLA. I call upon all Spanish subjects present to put this man in chains. (*Nothing happens.*) Put this man in chains, immediately.

COLUMBUS. You see? Nobody will dare touch me. If you can find one person who dares to put me in chains, I will not resist.

BOBADILLA. Is there no one here who'll follow the orders of the new viceroy Bobadilla, appointed by the King and Queen of Spain, to put this man in chains?

FRANCISCO. I'll do it.

COLUMBUS. What do you mean, you'll do it? We just made a deal.

FRANCISCO. (*Putting shackles on COLUMBUS, who stands there in shock and amazement, not resisting.*) I do not agree to chain you up in my capacity as colonist and slaveholder. Nor do I chain you up in my former capacity of revolutionary leader. I chain you up because I am ordered to do so by the new viceroy, because my first loyalty must always be to the King and Queen, and because for years I have cooked your food and you always moan and belch when you eat it. Italians do not understand good Spanish cooking. For this insult I gladly chain up this pompous baboon.

BOBADILLA. At last, I have finally found among you a man with some integrity.

TORQUEMADA. So the great Admiral of the Ocean Sea returned home from his third voyage in chains.

37 (Return of the Martyr)

The court of Spain. COLUMBUS is clanging around abysmally. The JESTER blows a fanfare and then follows him around making fun of him.

ISABELLA. Oh, for God's sake, Christopher, let us take off those chains. You look like Spartacus.

COLUMBUS. I've worn them all the way across the Atlantic, I must wear them now, they suit me. This is the reward I get for serving your majesties so loyally, I'm put in chains and shipped to Spain like a common criminal, like some—

PROSECUTOR. Slave?
COLUMBUS. Slave. Yes. Like some, some—
PROSECUTOR. Indian?

(HE looks at the PROSECUTOR, who stares back.)

ISABELLA. We never told them to put you in chains.
We had so many complaints and rumors of insurrection in
Hispaniola we felt compelled to send out a new governor to
investigate, and we needed you here so you could answer
your accusers in person. Nobody wanted chains, it was a
mistake.
COLUMBUS. But you've taken my titles away from
me.
ISABELLA. Nonsense. You can have your titles.
COLUMBUS. You've taken my governorship away.
FERDINAND. You were a terrible governor.
COLUMBUS. You've taken my riches from me.
FERDINAND. That belongs to us, not you. You work
for us, remember?
ISABELLA. We've decided to grant you a castle of your
own, and a very generous pension on which to retire.
JUANA. It's nice, I've seen it, you can raise goats and
fish in the moat. We can play tag in the nude.
COLUMBUS. I don't want a castle, I don't want a
pension and I don't want goats. I am the Admiral of the
Ocean Sea. I want my ocean back. I can't end my career in
chains. If you'll just let me go back one more time I'll find
the Emperor of China and end in a glorious triumph, not
like this, oh, please, I beg you—

FERDINAND. This is pathetic, I'm going to bed. Are you coming?

COLUMBUS. NO.

FERDINAND. Not you, her.

COLUMBUS. (*Grabbing onto the King's leg.*) I can't let you go until I get another voyage.

ISABELLA. (*Pulling him away hastily.*) You go on to bed, dear. I'll speak to Christopher. Go on. I'll be in later and bring you something hot.

(*FERDINAND points to Columbus, makes a circle around his ear with his finger to indicate that Columbus is insane, and goes. ISABELLA looks at COLUMBUS, who sits down and begins to cry.*)

ISABELLA. Oh, don't cry. I'll convince him to send you back, but not as governor of anything, your talents do not lie in that direction. You may have one more voyage of exploration and discovery. But just one.

COLUMBUS. I don't want your pity.

ISABELLA. I know, you want my money. And that's just what you're getting. So take it and run, life is short. And this is your last chance.

38 (The Last Voyage)

TORQUEMADA. So you got your last voyage.

COLUMBUS. (*Taking off chains and throwing them away as he speaks.*) I got more than that. God vindicated me on my fourth voyage. He gave me a sign that he was still on my side, by punishing my enemies.

TORQUEMADA. Did he?

COLUMBUS. When I returned to Hispaniola I found that ass, Bobadilla, getting ready to sail back to Spain.

BOBADILLA. What's your problem now, Admiral?

COLUMBUS. I must speak to you, it's very important.

BOBADILLA. Aren't you supposed to be looking for China?

COLUMBUS. We had to put in here, there was no choice.

BOBADILLA. Why? Giant crabs? It's a beautiful day.

COLUMBUS. There's going to be a terrible storm.

BOBADILLA. Oh, so now the great Admiral of the Ocean Slop can predict the weather, too?

COLUMBUS. You've got to let us stay and ride out the storm, and you must on no account try to head back to Spain until the tempest is over.

BOBADILLA. Did God tell you about this tempest? Or did your dead wife come to you in a vision?

COLUMBUS. Listen to me, you blockhead. I've been through two such tempests in this part of the world, and I know the signs. The seals and manatees are coming to the surface—

BOBADILLA. The seals and the manatees tell you what the weather's going to be, do they?

COLUMBUS. Please, just wait one day. If there's no tempest, then you can all laugh at me.

BOBADILLA. We're already laughing at you. Now get out of my harbor, or I'll arrest you and bring you back in chains again. Seals and manatees. Jesus wept.

COLUMBUS. So I found another harbor and he sailed for Spain. The hurricane sank nineteen ships with no survivors. God vindicated me on that day.

PROSECUTOR. And you took great pleasure in it.

COLUMBUS. I was gratified, yes.

PROSECUTOR. You were gratified by the deaths of hundreds of men.

COLUMBUS. No, not by that—

PROSECUTOR. You put your own personal vanity above your concern for those creatures, as always.

COLUMBUS. I tried to warn them. What could I do?

PROSECUTOR. And you felt triumphant.

COLUMBUS. I deserved to feel triumphant. My fourth voyage was a great triumph. I discovered gold in Panama—

PROSECUTOR. And were driven out by the natives.

COLUMBUS. We fought them valiantly—

PROSECUTOR. The only valiant member of your party was a large dog. And the climax of your triumphs was to be shipwrecked on Jamaica. If somebody hadn't stumbled upon you by accident, you'd have died there. You ended as you began, a shipwrecked sailor, sea wrack, washed up on shore, nothing.

COLUMBUS. But that wasn't the end. I was rescued, and returned to Spain to see the Queen.

39 (China Discovered)

The court. JUANA alone, playing with the Jester's horn.

JUANA. Christopher! Oh, give me a big kiss. I missed you.

COLUMBUS. Thank you, your highness, but where is everybody? I need to see the Queen.

JUANA. You can't see her.

COLUMBUS. But I've got to.

JUANA. Well, you can't. They've buried her.

COLUMBUS. They buried the Queen?

JUANA. She left them no choice. She died.

COLUMBUS. The Queen is dead?

JUANA. If she's not, I'll bet she's really furious down there.

COLUMBUS. Oh, God. Then I must see the King.

JUANA. He's left orders never to let you anywhere near him.

COLUMBUS. But I've got to get ships for my next voyage. My revenues. My emoluments. My share of the gold.

JUANA. Thank you for your sympathy, Christopher.

COLUMBUS. I'm sorry, I'm sorry, it hasn't sunk in yet, my mind has been on fire. I loved the Queen.

JUANA. I know, but Daddy thinks you're crazy and he won't see you.

COLUMBUS. Then how am I going to get more ships? I've still got to find the Emperor of China, and my brain is burning, it's burning. You don't think I really AM crazy, do you?

JUANA. I'm not sure I'm the best person to ask, Christopher. The study of Latin and sexual intercourse have left me insane, amo, amas, amat, and I'm grateful to you and Julius Caesar for this. My mother had ten children, and they all died but me, and I was the one she liked the least. I married Philip the Handsome, and gave birth to Emperors, but he loved other women, and when Mother died I became the Queen of Hearts, but Father rules for me, while I stay in the palace, running around naked and visiting the grave of my husband, who has become a very prosperous worm farm. I have sex with my dead husband's ghost in the cemetery. He's a much better lover now that he's dead, but I think he betrays me with the other corpses. What was the question again?

COLUMBUS. Do you think I'm insane?

JUANA. This is something I've thought seriously about. The thing is, there's different kinds of madness. There's the more common, destructive madness, that distorted and unorthodox way of looking at the world which results in tyranny and violence, physical and psychological, to others and to one's self. Then there's the much more rare, creative madness, that distorted and unorthodox way of looking at the world which results in creation, exploration and discovery. The problem is that to ordinary, normal people, they look like pretty much the same thing, which is why some of the best books and people in the world tend to get thrown on bonfires. Myself, I travel through my insanity as on a wondrous voyage. Perhaps you should be that kind of explorer, Christopher—instead of sailing back and forth across the ocean, go inside your ears. It's much more satisfying in your head, the possibilities are infinite, and you don't have to worry so much about barnacles.

COLUMBUS. No, I can't do that, I need more ships, I need to see the dead Queen, my head is on fire, I must go back again across the water. Where are the Chinese? Have they torn down all the pagodas just to frustrate me? This China is a very confusing place. I don't want to make voyages in my head. It's burning in there. I want to find the Emperor of China.

JUANA. Maybe you're looking in the wrong place. Maybe you haven't found China because you've found someplace else entirely. You've found the United States of Vespucci.

COLUMBUS. I have NOT found someplace else. How could it DARE be someplace else? You mustn't presume I didn't find China just because I had a little trouble locating any Chinese. These Orientals are very tricky people, that's why they call it the mysterious east. I know the Emperor of China is around here somewhere. Where is he? Is he dining with the dead Queen? Is he hiding? I demand to see the Emperor.

(A loud GONG is heard. Three beautiful CHINESE GIRLS appear.)

COLUMBUS. At last. I knew it. Look. Chinese women. They're even more beautiful than Pinzon said. How did he know? Please, I must see the Emperor at once.

FIRST CHINESE GIRL. He's coming now.

SECOND CHINESE GIRL. He's been dying to see you.

THIRD CHINESE GIRL. He wonders what took you so long.

FIRST CHINESE GIRL. He has a golden mountain to give you.

SECOND CHINESE GIRL. A thousand slave girls, each more beautiful than the next, will take baths with you.

THIRD CHINESE GIRL. The Emperor will adopt you as his son and heir, and then politely expire.

FIRST CHINESE GIRL. Here he comes.

SECOND CHINESE GIRL. Stand up.

THIRD CHINESE GIRL. Sit down.

FIRST CHINESE GIRL. Bow.

SECOND CHINESE GIRL. Curtsey.

THIRD CHINESE GIRL. Roll over.

FIRST CHINESE GIRL. Bark.

SECOND CHINESE GIRL. Play dead.

THIRD CHINESE GIRL. Cover your eyes.

(The GONG again. COLUMBUS has been trying desperately to follow these orders, and is now on his back, holding his eyes. The EMPEROR of China appears.)

EMPEROR. What's that? Another dead eunuch? Get rid of him.

COLUMBUS. *(Alarmed, jumping up.)* Oh, your majesty, I am not a dead eunuch, I`am the Admiral of the Ocean Sea, and I am honored to greet the Great Emperor of China at last.

EMPEROR. Who?

COLUMBUS. I am Christopher Columbus, and I've been searching for you all my life. My Emperor, I bring greetings from King Ferdinand and the dead Queen Isabella of Spain.

EMPEROR. Who?

COLUMBUS. The King and Queen of Spain, your inscrutableship, the greatest monarchs in all the world.

EMPEROR. You silly person, I am the greatest monarch in the world, and I don't want to hear about the squabbles of your petty little primitive tribal chieftains in Europe. Unless of course they might make good slaves. We can always use good slaves.

COLUMBUS. But your majesty, what about my golden mountain? What about the thousand maidens? Am I not to be your son and heir?

EMPEROR. Are you kidding? He's kidding, right?

COLUMBUS. But then why, after all these years of searching for you, after all this humiliation and suffering, why have you finally granted me an audience?

EMPEROR Because you're hallucinating, you gonad. There are no dancing girls here, there is no Emperor. I'm a delusion. You are actually at the bottom of the sea, and we are all sea lions.

(*The EMPEROR and the CHINESE GIRLS all slap their arms together like flippers and bark like sea lions.*)

EMPEROR. You have drowned in the consequences of your own madness, in the ocean inside your head, and you will be lost forever in the burning water.

COLUMBUS. That isn't true. You're not the Emperor of China. You're the Devil. You've been sent by God to torment me. But I will not be tormented. Could I please have one of these girls to take home and show the dead Queen?

EMPEROR. What's that smell? Is it him? God, these Europeans smell like dead fish. Get him away from me. Take him out in the square and run over him with wagons. Better yet, let him live, just ignore him.

COLUMBUS. No, not that. Not that. You can't do that.

(The GONG sounds again. The stage DARKENS. Then—)

40 (Judgement)

Eerie RED LIGHT up on TORQUEMADA, up on the shipwreck with a large black book.

TORQUEMADA. Columbus. Sir. Admiral. Pay attention, I'm about to render a judgement.

COLUMBUS. A judgement? Do I get to make another voyage? Will you give me more ships?

TORQUEMADA. In the matter of the immortal soul of one Christopher Columbus, this Inquisition finds as follows: the subject has committed sins of lechery and pride, rather more than most. But on the other hand, he has greatly reduced the number of savage and non-Christian persons living in the world, and brought under the Spanish flag vast new territories which will prove to the greater glory of God and his church. He will therefore remain in Purgatory for a few hundred years, expiating his sins of lechery and pride, and then be admitted to the kingdom of the blessed in Heaven.

PROSECUTOR. What about the enslavement and genocide of two continents full of human beings? Does that mean nothing?

TORQUEMADA. It is no disgrace to be a slave. In the Bible there are many slaves held by God's chosen. The important thing is the state of one's soul. Secondly, can we call these creatures true human beings until they've become Christians? And how can they become Christians unless we can teach them? And how can we make them listen to us if we do not control them? And how can we afford to go back and forth across the ocean to save their souls if we are not making some profit from this? It is my judgement that God permits us to enslave the heathen so we can save them. And since their bodies belong to God, it is an illusion that one man can own another in the first place. Thus it is not just permissible for us to enslave our fellow men, it is our Christian duty, and for this we commend the Admiral. Good work. Now, if you'll excuse me, I have another shipment of Jews to deal with. Good day, and congratulations. (*HE closes his book, turns and leaves.*)

COLUMBUS. (*Looking around at the other people, who stand watching him.*) Well? You see? I'm not to be blamed for what happened to the savages. My crimes of lechery and pride I can expiate in Purgatory. I shall be in

Heaven. I am a great man. I've done incredible things. So why do you all look at me like that?

(The PEOPLE begin one by one to turn their backs on him and leave.)

COLUMBUS. Where are you going? I have made great discoveries. I have made investigations into truth. I have sailed into the mouth of truth, I have loved truth and believed in truth and lived my truth and triumphed in truth. They will never forget me. I will be the king of the history books. I will live on when those who have slandered and abused me are rotting in boxes or under the sea. How dare you turn your backs on me. *(MUSIC up softly.)* Don't you know who I am? Do you you condemn me for a few piddling savages? When the Grand Inquisitor himself has absolved me? The voice of authority absolves me. I am the man who went east by sailing west. I am the solver of all paradoxes. Why do you turn away from me? Don't you understand?

(LIGHT closing in on him. FELIPA, then BEATRIZ, and finally the PROSECUTOR have been the last to leave. Only JUANA remains.)

COLUMBUS. I am the man who sailed west to China! I am the man who sailed west to China!

(HE sits down in the middle of the shipwreck and holds his head in despair. JUANA looks at him, starts to go, hesitates. Then SHE sighs, moves back towards him,

sits down beside him, rests his head against her breasts and comforts him. The LIGHT fades out and the MUSIC ends. Just the sound of OCEAN and GULLS in the darkness.)

End of Play

NOTES

In the nineteenth century, Washington Irving, the creator of Rip Van Winkle and Ichabod Crane, wrote an enormously popular and charming three volume biography of Columbus which collected and perpetuated all of the anecdotes and legends that our grandparents grew up believing, and which presented the mad Italian sailor as a wise and benign epic hero. In the twentieth century, Samuel Eliot Morison wrote a considerably less fanciful but nearly as adulatory biography which became the standard work on Columbus for many years. But in recent decades, revisionist historians have been systematically demolishing the myth of the great man and replacing it with dark portraits of a vicious, satanic monster who introduced slavery to the new world, slaughtered its inhabitants and raped its environment. Some of these historians have overt political and social agendas of their own to promote and defend. Others profess to wish simply to expose and correct the lies and distortions which have been perpetuated through the centuries by a series of white, male, western establishment historians whose own political agendas and prejudices were just as deeply ingrained in their work.

A playwright is neither a historian nor an editorial writer, but he makes his own investigations into truth, explorations which are no less inherently significant—in the hundred years after Columbus the most complex, powerful and enduring writing in western civilization was done not by a historian or a political polemicist but by an English playwright named Shakespeare. Yet when confronted with this vast body of exciting, contradictory, confusing, pompous, shrill, fatuous, compelling, vitriolic, tragic, funny and self-serving literature about Columbus, I began to wonder if the real human being who once must have lived, breathed, laughed, cried, made love, hated, feared and despaired must by now be so impossibly smothered by this five hundred year avalanche of mixed adoration and calumny that he could never be found again. A playwright deals not in abstractions but in the particular—it is through the paying of a certain kind of passionate attention to the particular that the playwright arrives at larger issues. A play is a poem of flesh and blood that moves. Through the flesh and blood of the actors one struggles backwards towards some vision of what it might have felt like to be this person, before this incredible barrage of wish-fulfillment and self-righteous hindsight had fallen upon him.

There are some disadvantages to working in this particular art form. One is limited by the amount of time the human posterior can tolerate being pressed against a theatre seat, by the capacity of the human bladder, and by the fickle and capricious human attention span. A playwright is also limited by his own experience and prejudices—one is Italian, so one is inclined to be sympathetic to Italians. One is devoting one's life to an impossible task, to create a serious and enduring body of dramatic literature in a time and a society which does not value theatre, does not see a play as literature unless the playwright has the good fortune to be a dead European, and rewards the mediocre and the stupid as it censors and destroys the rest—so one finds one's self tremendously sympathetic to a man confronted at every turn by hostile and contemptuous authority figures and obsessed by doing an even more insanely impossible thing—sailing west to get to the east. And thus from one's own welter of contradictory emotions and experience life is gradually breathed into a character—not the playwright, not the actor, not the audience, not Columbus, and not what has been written by others about him, but a complex amalgamation of all these which, if the gods are kind on a given night, becomes through the strange alchemy of theatre in some sense real, real enough at least to make us laugh or cry, identify with his struggles, make his mistakes with him, have his adventures, love his women, commit his crimes, and share his guilt.

Theatre is much more important than praise or blame. Theatre is a way of generating a powerful and complex illusion, a set of lies that creates in the mind of the watcher a complex emotional experience, a certain sense of communion with the characters, the actors, and the other watchers, and the ambiguous and disturbing presence of the ghost of something like truth.

Possible hypothetical no doubt deeply flawed chronology of the mad Italian sailor's life:

1451 Born in Genoa, Italy, between August and October, son of Domenico and Susanna Colombo. Domenico was a wool weaver. The dialect of Genoa was almost incomprehensible to other Italians. Problems of communication were to plague him. The person who does not speak the native language well always tends to look, to stupid people, like a fool.

1464 Begins going on voyages for his father's business, age 13. Observing the complex negotiations of merchants and traders on these voyages, the young Columbus begins to develop his own accomplished line of bull. This will serve him well later on.

1473 Sails to Chios, age 22. Studies maps, Pliny the Elder, Marco Polo. Observing how difficult the Turks and others have made the old overland trade routes to the east, he begins to develop his idea about sailing west to get there. At some point, this idea turns to an obsession.

1476 Shipwrecked, swims ashore at Lagos, Portugal, and makes his way to Lisbon. Perhaps this never happened. He is 25.

1477 Visit to Iceland. Age 26. Did he gather stories about the voyages of Leif Erikson to Vinland, nearly five hundred years earlier? Leif Erikson was as far in the past to Columbus as Columbus is to us.

1479 Marries Felipa. Age 28. Presumably it was no accident that her family owned ships. They live happily on an island.

1485 Prince John of Portugal refuses to fund his voyage west. Death of his wife. He is now 34, widowed, with a little boy to take care of, and no one is interested in his plan.

1486 He tries his luck in Spain. Meets his friend Diego, who introduces him to Diego's orphaned cousin Beatriz, who becomes the mad Italian sailor's mistress. She knows somebody who knows the Marquesa de Moya, who can arrange a meeting with the Queen. Observe that

Columbus has much better success with women than with men. No male authority figure trusts him, but at each step along his way, a woman helps him. On May 1 he gets his first audience with Queen Isabella. He is not yet 35. It will take him six long years of waiting, begging, and fuming, being nice to pompous idiots, before he gets what he wants.

1488 Beatriz gives birth to his second son. Columbus is now 37 and still waiting for word from Ferdinand and Isabella. This long period of frustration and humiliation explains much of his impatience and anger later in his life. He is a man whose patience has been pushed beyond endurance, and when he gets his voyages, he will be so anxious to get things done that he will lose all sense of the consequences of his actions.

1492 After much struggle, Columbus finally sails from Palos on his first voyage, August 3. He is nearly 41.

October 12, 2 AM: Rodrigo sights land.

October 28: Cuba.

December 5: Haiti (Hispaniola).

December 24: The *Santa Maria* is wrecked on a coral reef while Columbus and his crew are having a Christmas Eve celebration with the natives on shore. This image of his flagship wrecked on the reef will linger in his head, come back to him on his deathbed, and become the geography of his last hallucination and thus of this play. It is the wreckage of his life.

1493 January 16: begins his journey back to Spain.

March 15: sails into Palos.

September 25: sails out again on second voyage.

1494 June: returns to Spain from second voyage. He is nearly 43. He is beginning to wonder why he hasn't been able to find any Chinese people in what he still believes is China. He will go to his grave having no idea what he has actually found.

1498 Third voyage. Age 47. Columbus is put into chains and sent back to Spain in disgrace. He is a terrible governor. But because Ferdinand and Isabella are concerned about the advances that other countries have made in this area, they will eventually be persuaded to send him back again. His return in chains was in 1500.

1502 His fourth and last voyage. He is 51. The entire fleet is lost, and Columbus is shipwrecked in Jamaica.

1504 Columbus is rescued and returns home to Spain. Age 53. Queen Isabella has died, and Ferdinand refuses to see him.

1506 May 20, Columbus dies, broken and furious, still trying to see Ferdinand, and still convinced that he'd sailed west to China. He is not yet 55. His life has been a triumphant disaster.

Notes on certain other notable personages depicted in this play:

Torquemada (tawr kay MAH dah), Tomas de (1420-1498), first Inquisitor-General of Spain, born in Valladolid (where Columbus was to die), Dominican friar preacher there, then 22 years prior of the monastery of Santa Cruz at Segovia, confessor to Queen Isabella of Spain. Began work for the Inquisition in his late fifties, and in 1483 was appointed Inquisitor-General for all Spanish possessions.

Politically as well as religiously motivated, he probably thought the suppression of heretics would help unify Spain, which was still being won back from the Moors at this time. In 18 years as Inquisitor-General he saw to it that at least two thousand persons were executed for heresy, most of them strangled and burned. Even the Pope was disturbed by his severity. Torquemada was largely responsible for the driving out of 800,000 Jews from Spain, and for the theft of all their land, other property and finances. Spain never recovered from the loss of these people, who as a class tended to be the most educated and prosperous. Hated and feared, he was always heavily guarded. The Inquisition had tremendous, nearly unlimited powers. Ferdinand and Isabella needed money desperately and used the Inquisition to steal from the Jews. It was not officially abolished until 1834, but its official name, the Congregation of the Holy Office, lingered on to keep the Index of Prohibited Books. Thus we observe the long relationship that religious bigotry, book burning and censorship have had with each other. Religions tend to grow bigots, and bigots need heretics to persecute. There is a direct line of descent from the reasoning of the Inquisition to the reasoning of Hitler, to the reasoning of contemporary religious and political fanatics and advocates of censorship. The Inquisition is alive and well and living in Cincinnati, putting directors of art museums in jail. Five hundred years after Columbus, a person can still be persecuted, jailed and executed for writing a book, painting a picture, daring to think and create, to make his own investigations into truth.

Beatriz Enriquez de Harana, mother of Columbus's second son, met him when she was twenty, he in his mid-thirties. Her family made wine near Cordoba. Orphaned, she was taken in by her father's brother, and grew up with her cousin Diego, the friend of Columbus. She could read and write. She was still living when Columbus died, but did not come to his funeral. A year before his death, Columbus wrote his son by Felipa to please take good care of Beatriz, "for she weighs heavily upon my conscience, though at present I am unable to say why."

The marriage of Isabella (1451-1504) of Castile to her cousin Ferdinand (1452-1516) of Aragon was a political triumph, as it cleared the way for a united, Christian Spain, after centuries of Moorish rule that had been gradually pushed south until the last Moorish stronghold fell with the capture of Granada in 1492. Isabella was beautiful, intelligent, much beloved by her people, and in private warm and open. She was personally courageous and worked hard all her life to be a good sovereign. It was unfortunately part of her diligence both as a Christian and a monarch that she supported the Inquisition of her old confessor Torquemada, and used it for her purposes. Her husband Ferdinand was a much colder and more cynical pragmatist (Machiavelli thought him the perfect monarch), who cheated on his wife and was tolerated by the people only for her sake. He was very efficient, punishing blasphemy by cutting out tongues, and was a cunning diplomat. Once castigated by the King of France for having deceived him twice, Ferdinand responded that the King of France was a liar, that in fact Ferdinand had deceived him at least ten times. They greatly reduced highway robbery,

reformed the judiciary, ended many abuses of the
aristocracy, and ended the chaos that had plagued divided
Spain. They also deported eight hundred thousand Jews and
stole everything they had. Ferdinand disliked and distrusted
Columbus, but tolerated him because Isabella liked and
believed in him. After the Queen's death, Columbus was
out in the cold permanently. They had ten children, all of
whom died fairly young except the mad Princess Juana.

Princess Juana la Loca, also known as Joanna the Mad,
was to be the mother of the Emperor Charles V and the
grandmother of King Philip II of Spain, he of the Spanish
Armada. When she had the hair of her husband's mistress
cut off, he swore he would never sleep with Juana again. It
is said that her grief over her daughter's marital problems
hastened Isabella's death. She lived on until 1555, but
never left her palace after 1507, wandering around naked and
staring out the window at the grave of her dead husband.
Years after Isabella and Ferdinand were dead, a rebellion of
nobles took place, Juana's palace was captured, and Juana
was taken hostage. The leader of the rebellious nobles tried
every way he knew how to get the insane Juana to sign a
document that would depose her son Charles and name
herself as Queen. Juana was crazy but she was not stupid.
She told them to drop dead. There is no evidence that the
real Juana ever met Columbus, and in fact the history
books say her marriage did not occur until 1496, but who
are you going to believe? Fifty thousand painstaking
historians, or me? For those unfortunate persons who must
have a rational explanation, we could say that in his dying
delirium, Columbus imagined himself to have been a great
friend of Juana because he identified so strongly,

subconsciously, with her position of looney outsider. A play is not a history book. It has its own truth.

Felipa, the very young wife of Columbus, was a Perestrello on her father's side—the Perestrellos were Italians who emigrated to Portugal in the 1300s—and a Moniz on her mother's side. Her father had been trained as a captain and explorer by Henry the Navigator, and became a wealthy governor. When her father died, her mother and the Moniz family took over his affairs. Her bad-tempered and possessive uncle Moniz probably existed, although I don't know that for a fact. She did meet Columbus in church, and did honeymoon on the island of Porto Santo, which had belonged to her father.

The self-important viceroy Bobadilla existed, and did put Columbus in chains. Captain Martin Alonso Pinzon was in fact probably a much more respectable person than in this play. He did abandon Columbus on the first voyage, rejoined him for the return to Spain, then deserted him again in a desperate attempt to get to Ferdinand and Isabella first, but they refused to see him, preferring to wait for Columbus to get there. Pinzon died shortly afterwards. The Vivaldis were apparently real, as were Rodrigo—who is said to have hanged himself in his despair at not getting the reward, Prince John, who apparently was in fact a cold, sardonic individual, and of course Vespucci. The Marquesa de Moya also existed, and there are many rumors about her affair with Columbus. Dr. Slawkenbergius bears the name of a fellow mentioned in one of my own personal holy books, *The Life and Opinions of Tristram Shandy, Gentleman*, in which, as I remember it, anyway, he tells the very edifying story of the stranger with the enormous nose.

Excerpts from the playwright's notebook:

All statements about Columbus could be lies. The books disagree violently about many things. Some write to worship. Others write to attack. It is always much more difficult and less popular to try and understand without frantic attempts to deny the fundamental ambiguity inherent in all human endeavors. People who have done wonderful, brave things are generally also, given the right circumstances, capable of doing hideous things. This does not mean that they are monsters. All human actions have consequences unforeseen and undesired by those who act. This does not release us from responsibility for our actions. Do not make excuses for murderers. But look in the mirror. All writing, like all human activity, is horribly compromised. The brave struggle against this and fail. That is what art is about.

The compass always seeks the truth. Go south until the butter melts, then west. The ship's log is a way of keeping sane. I write to keep sane. Yet the act of writing itself, not casual writing but obsessive, unquenchable writing, day by day, week by week, year by year, that characterizes the genuine heroes, Shakespeare, Yeats, Joyce, Eliot, Faulkner, without praise, without comfort, irrespective of external reward, which is at best a trap, this unreasonable commitment is also often considered by persons who cannot understand it to be insane behavior, or, to the religious bigots among you, possession by some demon.

The irony is that in fact it does feel a bit like some sort of demonic possession. And yet it is the holy state. The sea of darkness surrounds the mariner. I am devoured by a big fish, a sea serpent, satan in the water. He links the middle ages to the renaissance. History puts us into boxes. He is being crushed to death between two ages like a gnat between the pages of a history book. We betray history by writing about it, even as we attempt to be true to it. We distort and destroy by interpreting, and the very act of writing is an interpretation and a compromise. We are limited by our ignorance and our prejudices. All we can do is trust the imaginary god inside us to be the compass which always seeks the truth. Sometimes the god within lies. This is destructive madness. All creation breeds destruction. This is the horror of the creator. God plants the garden and then regrets it. And yet, despite everything, one chooses to create, to make these investigations into truth. That is the kind of monkey one is.

The American theatre: the mediocre trying to coax the bored to worship the stupid. Greedy, cowardly, pompous, vicious. My home. Step out onto an empty stage and all that disappears, and once again something holy happens. A post the passing dogs defile, Yeats said. All the church I have.

He was named for Saint Christopher, the patron saint of travellers. Now and then God makes a little joke to deceive us into suspecting that he exists.

New York: a place where good actors, bad directors and hideously mangled plays go to be killed.

Script development: people who can't write engaged in a friendly endeavor to destroy the work of people who can. See also, dramaturgy, critic.

Hell: a place where adjudicators sit around adjudicating each other's adjudications.

Broadway: the elephants' burial ground, with tap dancing. See also whorehouse, cannibalism, death rattle.

While he waited for six years, from 1486 to 1492, for a firm answer, Isabella took pity on Columbus and gave him some money to buy a few decent clothes and a mule. The mule, I suppose, was for love interest.

Everything that happens in rehearsal shows up sooner or later, for better or worse, in the performance. Everything.

The play is the soul, the production the body, the play moves from production to production like the soul moves from body to body in Hindu mythology.

The way a play moves is always a part of the play. Every transition is a part of the play. There are no empty spaces.

We collaborate on the production, we don't collaborate on the play. I write the play.

A play is a poem of flesh and blood that moves.

A play is a work of literature. A novel is a work of literature meant to be read and imagined in the mind of the reader. A play is a work of literature meant to be read and imagined in the mind of the reader, then made flesh on a stage with actors. When the audience sees the play, they imagine its world in their heads. The novel simply cuts out the middle men. But I like the middle men. The middle women. The mess of the theatre. Theatre is flesh and blood.

In this play the actors must learn to play well without the ball—that is, when they are onstage but without lines in a given scene, in another time or place, but still visible and animated. Everything onstage must be connected to everything else, and psychological threads connect characters across the stage and across time and space. The texture of this universe is and must be constantly changing and alive. What we are seeing is psychological reality— you can connect across time and space because you are alive in each other's minds. Everybody onstage is just as real as everybody else. Unless a player must be offstage in a given scene to change into somebody else, or for some other very good reason, such as to set up another entrance, the player will be onstage and visible, playing without the ball.

Dramatic action is not something that happens on a stage, it is something that happens in the mind of the audience. What happens on the stage is what causes a dramatic action to happen in the mind of the perceiver. A sword fight may be generating no dramatic action whatsoever, while a simple conversation between two actors sitting in chairs on an otherwise bare stage may be generating tremendous dramatic action. What matters is what the play makes happen in the mind of the perceiver.

Every play is a mystery. We are the detectives, we assemble the clues left for us by the playwright and attempt to solve the mystery. In a great play, we fail, but are so intrigued and compelled that we return to fail again and again.

Trust the play. Trust the words. Memorize the exact word, or you will foul up the rhythms of the play. Timing is everything. Never try to impose a layer of style or cleverness between the audience and the play. You are not here to show everybody how good you are. Trust the play. A director who does not trust the play should not be directing it.

The idea of sailing west to get to the east did not originate with Columbus. It had been talked about since the days of the Roman Empire. But to the best knowledge of anyone in Columbus's time, no one had successfully done it. In the end, like all explorers and creators he is left with the incomprehension of those who would judge him, the terrible consequences of his own actions, his own failure to understand himself, and his madness.

Notes on costumes

They should be as simple as possible, very easy to get in and out of, and very easy to move around in. The actors will be all over the set, up and down steps and platforms, up in the crow's nest, on the floor, running about, in every conceivable position. The essence of this production style should be constant, gradual movement, a continuously evolving picture. Presume that every actor will in the course of the play be everywhere and do everything, and this is as true for the female characters as for the men. In most cases one flexible costume for each character. Sacrifice historical accuracy for flexibility and ease of movement in every case. This is not costume drama. The moving actor is central. Whatever facilitates ease of movement, simple transitions and quick changes is good. Whatever makes these things difficult is the wrong choice. In most cases the actors should only be offstage as long as it takes them to change their costumes. Otherwise, they will be onstage, visible and in character all the time. It is imperative that nothing be too difficult to get in and out of. Colors: dark. Browns. Wine colors. Blood red here and there. Black for Torquemada. Creamy white for Felipa. Dark blues. Nothing bright. Even the King and Queen dress fairly simply. Footwear must be comfortable and compatible with climbing, running, jumping, and we must minimize clunking with all this movement. The Native Girls wear body suits with sarongs or strategic patches to look like body paint. There should be no actual nudity. The crocodile hand puppet Maurice should look much like Kukla and Fran's pal Ollie. A crow for the Crow Woman. A pig for the Pig Woman. The two-headed costume with punching bag heads must be constructed, of course. The Mermaids should appear from out of the shipwreck structure in their rather dark scene in a way that conceals the fact that they can walk in their costumes. When they press their legs together, toe to toe, they should appear to be fish from waist down, with apparently seamless, lovely tails. The long shirt of Columbus should double as a nightshirt. His boots and pants should be easy to get on and off. Desdemona's screamer doll is a rag doll the hands of which form a necklace for Desdemona, thumbs connected in front, forefingers snap together at back, the whole doll when extended as long as Desdemona's arms, so that when she is in the grip of her mania, she can grab its little feet and pull out, arms fully extended, so it appears to be a little person strangling her, and then when she feels better she can let it hang there as a bizarre necklace, or play with it like a regular doll, pulling up its little dress so that it can flash the King, or doing other annoying things with it. The crow, the crocodile puppet, the doll and the pig should all be treated as real people.

The following costume plots were prepared by Susan
Brown for the first production of *Mariner:*

MEN'S COSTUME PLOT

Character	Act/Sc	Type of Costume
Torquemada 1	I & II	Long sleeveless robe, tights, hat
Columbus 1	I & II	Doublet, breeches, sleeveless gown, hat, boots
Moniz 1	I, 1-11; II, 40	Doublet, robe
Bobadilla 2	I, 15-20; II, 27-30	Foppish hat, doublet, breeches
Pinzon 3	II, 21-25	Breeches, vest, shirt, hat
Rodrigo 1	I, 1-3; II, 21-25, 40	"Sailor" breeches, shirt, sash, cap
Headless 2	I, 6	Coat over Rodrigo
Jester 3	I, 10-20; II, 27-37	Jester tunic/hat
Beggar 1	I, 1-3; II, 21-25, 40	Ragged shirt/pants
Slawkenbergius 2	I, 6-11	Houppelande, hat
Ferdinand 3	I, 15-20; II, 27-37	Rich doublet/crown
Diego 1	I, 1-3; 13-20; II, 21-26, 40	Doublet, breeches
Head 2	I, 6	2-head appliance
2nd Vivaldi 3	I, 9	Seaweed coat
Francisco 4	II, 30-37	Tabard, cowl
Ancient Mariner 1	I, 1-6, 13-20; II, 21-32, 40	Ragged coat, beard, hat, leggings
1st Vivaldi 2	I, 9	Seaweed coat
Vespucci 3	II, 35	Foppish doublet, hat, tights
Emperor 4	II, 39	Emperor robe
Dirty Carlos 1	I, 1-07, 13-17; II, 1-2	Breeches, shirt, vest, hat
Prince John 2	I, 9	Doublet, hat
Prosecutor 3	I, 20; II, 3-40	Monk's robe/cowl

WOMEN'S COSTUME PLOT

Character	Act/Sc	Type of Costume
Princess Juana 1	I & II	Laced dress, underskirt, crown
Lucinda 1	I, 1-3	Skirt, bodice, shirt
Desdemona 2	I, 6-20; II, 21-22, 40	New skirt, sleeves
3rd Native 3	II, 25-30	Body suit, sarong
3rd Mermaid 4	II, 34	Mermaid shirt, fins
3rd Chinese 5	II, 39	Mandarin coat, fan
Mama 1	I, 1-3	Laced dress, apron, hat
Pig Woman 2	I, 6-10; II, 21-22	Hood, overskirt
Isabella 3	I, 14-20; II, 27-40	Court dress, crown
Felipa 1	I & II	Overgown, gown, chemise, apron
Nurse 1	I, 1-11	Skirt, bodice, shirt, veiled headdress
Marquesa 2	I, 14-20; II, 26-40	Court gown, cut wig, headdress
Estrella 3	II, 1-2	Bodice, skirt, shirt
Beatriz 1	I, 1-3, 13-20; II, 24-40	Dress, chemise
Crow Woman 2	I, 6-10; II, 1-2	Skirt, blouse, cinch
Rosaura 1	I, 1-3, 14-20; II, 40	Court skirt, bodice sleeves, blouse
Crocodile Girl 2	I, 6-10; II, 21-22	Skirt
2nd Native 3	II, 25-30	See 3rd Native above
2nd Mermaid 4	Ii, 34	See 3rd Mermaid above
2nd Chinese 5	II, 39	See 3rd Chinese above
Maria 1	I, 1-20; II, 21-22; II, 40	Skirt, blouse, bodice
1st Native 2	II, 25-30	See 3rd Native above
1st Mermaid 3	II, 34	See above
1st Chinese 4	II, 39	See above

Notes on props for *Mariner*

Large black book to rest on upstage ship structure.
Blanket for bed should be dark and blend with set.
Simple wooden fishing pole for Ancient Mariner.
Dark pig bladder type ball, soccer size, for Lucinda.
Flower Columbus buys and gives to Juana.
Prop fish Juana produces from bosom, moderately floppy.
Knife Mama conceals in clothing.
Sausages and bread, edible.
Wooden plate.
Six wine bottles and six goblets.
Wooden soup bowl and spoon.
Small sword for Moniz.
Madhouse membership card for Juana.
The crow, pig, crocodile hand puppet and Desdemona's
    screamer doll should most likely be constructed by
    costume shop.
Prop head with flat bottom at neck—brought on by the
    Crow Woman, this is the Headless Man's head.
Pomegranate. Real if possible.
Loud, obnoxious, flatulent horn for Jester, and smaller
    version.
Whipped cream pie for Jester.
Shears for Juana.
Bag with dark clothing for Columbus to pack, stash under
    bed.
Popcorn in brown bag for Juana and Felipa to eat in crow's
    nest.
Coins for Columbus to bribe with.

Trinkets, beads, necklaces for sailors to trade with Native Girls.

Gold necklets, anklets, bracelets that Native Girls give sailors.

White bird glop for King to smash in face—whipped cream.

Dummy blunderbuss for King. No blanks, use two by four slap off.

Fake bird carcasses, sixteen or twenty, either bought or sewn stuffed animals from costume shop. No real birds, please. Ducks, parrots, cockatoos, gulls, and one or two strange looking things, a dodo, perhaps a penguin. Drop from above and perhaps hurl in arcs from sides to supplement. Bird hurling rehearsals required.

Pen for Columbus, quill.

Letter from Francisco's sister.

Chains and shackles for Columbus, chains should clank loudly, perhaps supplemented by sound. Also muzzles and shackles for Native Girls, must be easy for Juana to slip off them, perhaps costume rather than props.

Two wooden tables, four stools.

All props must be either preset or carried on and off by the actors. Nobody but actors onstage throughout, including intermission. It is helpful if the actors set their own props, as things will tend to migrate about the set in the course of the show, like the fish and the head, and the actors will know best where they need to be, and where they get to.

Notes on sound

Preshow: thirty minutes of opera, aural correlative to the Washington Irving view of Columbus. Theme for lead-in and out of the play, try Tom Waits, "Shiver Me Timbers" and "San Diego Serenade," both of which are on the *Heart of Saturday Night* and *Asylum Years* albums. Use live sound whenever possible. In the first production, two thundersheets, an old mechanical crank wind machine, a group of old pipes of various sizes hung from a rack and banged together for bells, and actors doing all manner of bird sounds, keening, singing, et cetera, a two by four whacked on the stage floor backstage for the gunshot, chains clanked on a tin sheet backstage to heighten the surreal clanking of Christopher's chains, all worked very well. This should be a rough, theatrical show, centered on actors and not technology. What follows is modified from the sound plot of sound designer Jim Knapp for this production:

Preshow
Verdi: Va, Pensiero (Nabucco)
Verdi: La Donna e Mobile (Rigoletto)
Bizet: Au Fond du Temple (Pearl Fishers)
Puccini: O Mio Babbino (Gianni Schicchi)
Puccini: Quando M'en Vo (La Boheme)
Delibes: Viens, Mallika (Lakme)
Leoncavallo: Vesti La Giubba (Pagliacci)
Lead-in
Shiver, from lights down, complete
Storm, Sc1

Live and tape
Gulls Sc2
Gentle coastal shore
Church bell Sc4
Cacophony: live
Island Sc8
Birds and ocean: live and tape
Storm Sc8
Storm brews, thunder: live and tape
Increases Sc9
Thunder, wind, rain: live and tape
Bell tolls Sc11
Ominous: live
Guitar Sc13
Cafe, Spanish
Wind Sc20
Ominous: live
Exit Sc20
San Diego: covers exit, lights down, plays through lights
    up and beginning of Intermission, which continues with
      Va, Pensiero, et cetera
Lead-in Sc21
Shiver, all but last two verses, covers actor entrances to
    tavern
Birds Sc27
Exotic jungle bird sounds: live and tape
Gunshot Sc27
Two by four whacked on floor: live
Chains Sc36
Heavy chains: live
Gong Sc39

Three Emperor gong cues: live
Exit Sc40
Shiver: last 2 verses, end of Columbus speech comes just
    before final verse, ocean/gulls/dark
CCall
San Diego: through lights up, curtain call
AudEx
Va, Pensiero, et cetera: begins after SD ends, exactly as at
    Intermission, play through until house empty

Notes on lighting

This should be a fairly dark show. A general wash and
many long, slow cross fades, with periodic evolutions into
thunderstorms, the shadows of flying birds effect, and more
demented hallucination effects as in the madhouse, the
Vivaldi and mermaid scenes, and elsewhere. Also, things
should gradually get darker and stranger as his mind begins
to turn through the second act. The thing to keep in mind
is that for most of this play, everybody and everything on
this stage is intimately connected to everybody and
everything else. We do not generally need or want areas too
sharply defined because no matter what scene is playing,
there will be people from other times and places onstage
and visible, in character and active, and times and places
will often interpenetrate. So we will have in any given
scene a major area of focus but we will also be able to see
people elsewhere. The thing to avoid is a sense of sudden
lights up here lights down there—except for special effects,
that will virtually never happen. Each scene flows
immediately into the next and often the people for the next

scene will already be in place before their scene starts, so all Columbus will have to do is turn around and look at somebody across the stage, and he will be in the scene with them. People will also sometimes play scenes from rather distant parts of the set, and at different levels. The essence of the play is the gradual and more or less continuous motion of actors. Often the light for the next area of focus will start creeping up slowly before the previous scene is done. Subtle, gradual, the light connects, it generally does not divide. The light is the play of his mind.

Notes on the set. Things to keep in mind:

(1) There need to be many, many places for actors to be.

(2) There need to be at least nine ways to get on and off the stage, and all backstage areas must be easily accessible to each other, so that an actor can go off DL and return UR very easily in costume without trauma.

(3) There need to be about five ways to get from any part of the set to any other part of the set easily and without traffic jams or costume worries. Example: if Rodrigo is UL on the ship, he should be able to get to his DR bottle on the table by going across the ship and down the R throne area, to the UC middle of the ship and down the main platform descent, then DR, down the L throne area to DL and across to DR, down the exit stairs UL, L, or UR and under the shipwreck structure, emerging at either R or L of the central staircase platforms, etc. The basic unit of this play is the easily moving actor with many options. Also, the many step units must be easily navigable by actors in shadowy situations—they will

always be in character, so they can't be watching their feet most of the time. Freedom of movement, easy access, sturdy, trusty footing. They will be all over this set, everybody, to every part of it, in every kind of costume. It will in terms of its use be like a giant wooden shipwreck jungle gym.

(4) There are no moving parts to this set except the wooden tables and stools that will mostly remain DR and DL and the sails that flap in the wind (hopefully we can do wind) on the broken masts of the ship upstage. The real moving parts are the actors.

(5) Every location on the shipwreck will at one time or another become more than one place, be used for a number of different things. What a place is will be determined almost entirely by what the actors are using it for. The motif is spewed out shipwreck trunks, boards, etc. on a reef. The throne structures only look like thrones when the king and queen are sitting in them. The rest of the time they are used as places to sit, fish from, stood on, or blend into the rest of the shipwreck. The function is always determined by the use the actor puts to it, thus we can't get too specific in detail. The bed, which in the shipwreck motif is the captain's bunk stuck on the reef, is connected to everything else. Everything is connected except the wooden tables and stools, and they should blend in very well, too. Use the picture of the Santa Maria as a starting point, but don't be afraid to distort. We are seeing Columbus's memory impression of the wreck, not what it must actually have been like. It is really the wreckage of his life.

Actor Tracks: interconnected road maps through *Mariner*
(Number at left refers to Scene)

Actor Track F1 (Juana)

1 Enters DL unhappy, throws stone in water, comforted, begins defense.
2 Watches from throne area and comments at end.
3 Watches with Torquemada.
4 In church with Torquemada.
5 Watches with Torquemada, shows her lifetime madhouse membership.
6 At home with madhouse people, swipes pomegranate, teases Torquemada
7 Watches proposal, finishes pomegranate, wipes hands on Torquemada
8 Observes from above bed.
9 Is appalled by the smell of the Vivaldis.
10 At Prince John's court, helps wipe pie off Columbus.
11 With Nurse and Torquemada at Felipa's death bed.
12 Comforts Nurse and helps her off.
13 At the Inn with Torquemada
14 Goes off briefly to get shears.
15 Chases Rosaura on, scene with Columbus, goes off, returns.
16 Sticks nose into King-Queen argument, follows them off to watch.
17 Off briefly to make next entrance.
18 Chases Marquesa with shears, scene with Isabella.
19 Watches from throne area.
20 At Spanish court, jumps in Christopher's arms. Intermission.
21 Observes Inn scene from crow's nest with Felipa.
22 Enjoys making fun of sailors at muster with other women.
23 In ocean dark during first voyage.
24 Tries to calm Columbus down, disturbed by Rodrigo's story.
25 Objects and is told to shut up.

26 Disturbed by references to butchering.

27 At court, loves birds, but very troubled by the muzzles.

28 Helps get muzzles off Native girls and makes friends with them.

29 Troubled by what she hears.

30 Upset by cannibalism.

31 Sympathy for Beatriz.

32 At Spanish court, asks about Beatriz.

33 With Beatriz during Felipa scene.

34 With Felipa during Mermaid scene.

35 Part of mad Vespucci chase.

36 Watches from upstage with Isabella.

37 At Spanish court, encourages Columbus to retire.

38 Observes sadly.

39 At court when he returns, tries to explain madness.

40 After others are gone, decides to go back and comfort him.

Actor Track F2 (Lucinda, Desdemona, 3rd Native, Mermaid, Chinese)

1 Lucinda

2 Lucinda

3 Lucinda

4 Off

5 Off

6 Desdemona at madhouse

7 Desdemona with Maria?

8 Desdemona

9 Desdemona

10 Desdemona at Portuguese court. Laughs.

11 Desdemona pursued by Jester?

12 Desdemona

13 Desdemona at inn.

14 Desdemona dumps Jester?

15 Desdemona

16 Desdemona observes with sympathy Maria & Diego

17 Desdemona with Maria?

18 Desdemona watches Maria & Diego?

19 Desdemona with Maria?

20 Desdemona
Intermission
21 Desdemona in the Palos Inn.
22 Desdemona makes fun of sailors.
23 Off
24 Off
25 3rd Native girl
26 3rd Native girl
27 3rd Native girl
28 3rd Native girl
29 3rd Native girl
30 3rd Native girl
31 Off
32 Off
33 Off
34 3rd Mermaid
35 Off
36 Off
37 Off
38 Off
39 3rd Chinese girl
40 Off briefly for quick change back to Desdemona, returns
   during Torquemada judgement

Actor Track F3 (Mama, Pig Woman, Isabella)
1 Mama
2 Mama
3 Mama
4 Off
5 Off
6 Pig Woman at madhouse.
7 Pig Woman
8 Pig Woman
9 Pig Woman
10 Pig Woman at Portuguese court.
11 Off
12 Off
13 Off

14 Isabella appears as mentioned.
15 Isabella at court.
16 Isabella
17 Off briefly
18 Isabella chases Juana on
19 Isabella sends Bobadilla to give message to Diego
20 Isabella at court
Intermission-change to Pig Woman
21 Pig Woman at the Inn. Pig drinking.
22 Pig Woman tries to join up for voyage.
23 Off changing back to Isabella
24 Off
25 Off
26 Off
27 Isabella, court scene.
28 Isabella
29 Isabella
30 Isabella
31 Isabella
32 Isabella, court scene
33 Isabella
34 Isabella
35 Isabella run down during Vespucci chase
36 Isabella
37 Isabella, court scene
38 Isabella dead
39 Isabella dead, observes from crow's nest
40 Isabella dead, leaves after judgement

Actor Track F4 (Felipa, Maid)
1 Felipa at the seashore.
2 Fussed over by the Nurse.
3 Getting ready for church with Nurse & Moniz R throne area.
4 At church with Nurse, finds Columbus.
5 In bed with Columbus, gets soup from Maria.
6 With Moniz and Nurse during madhouse, catching hell.
   Throws up.
7 Proposed to by the dragged back Columbus.

8 On Porto Santo with Columbus and Nurse.
9 Sleeping in bed with Columbus during Vivaldis.
10 Not feeling well, put to bed by Nurse.
11 Dead in bed, mourned by Nurse.
12 Felipa as Ghost, speaks with Columbus.
13 Watches as they speak of her.
14 Watches with Beatriz from close by.
15 Felipa
16 Felipa
17 Felipa
18 Felipa
19 Felipa
20 Felipa
Intermission
21 In crow's nest with Juana.
22 Observes muster.
23 On the bed during first voyage?
24 On bed with Beatriz during Rodrigo accusation?
25 Felipa
26 Felipa
27 Felipa
28 Felipa
29 Felipa
30 Felipa
31 Felipa as maid.
32 Felipa comforts Beatriz
33 Felipa talks to Columbus on Porto Santo
34 Felipa
35 Felipa
36 Felipa
37 Felipa
38 Felipa
39 Felipa
40 Felipa

Actor Track F5 (Nurse, Marquesa de Moya, Estrella)
1 Nurse scolds playing girls, is hit on head with ball.
2 Nurse fussing with Felipa's hair in R throne area.

3 With Felipa, getting ready to go to church.
4 With Felipa in church.
5 Trying to calm Moniz in Felipa's room.
6 With Felipa, tries to comfort her during madhouse. Discovers pregnancy.
7 With Felipa as Columbus is dragged back, angry at him.
8 Watches over Felipa & Columbus at Porto Santo.
9 Nurse in R throne sleeping, knitting? Do Vivaldis play with her?
10 Cares for the sick Felipa.
11 Weeping at Felipa's death bed.
12 Off changing to Marquesa de Moya.
13 Off
14 Marquesa de Moya appears as Beatriz speaks of her.
15 Marquesa at court, part of Rosaura/Juana encounter, off w/Diego?
16 Marquesa observes argument with Jester, has Margaret Dumont/Harpo rel.
17 Off getting bald wig.
18 Marquesa runs on half bald, chased by Juana.
19 Off briefly getting wig? to cover bald spot?
20 Marquesa at court, Jester in lap?
Intermission-changes to Estrella
21 Estrella with Pinzon at Inn
22 Estrella makes fun of sailors at muster
23 Off changing to Marquesa
24 Off
25 Off
26 Marquesa
27 Marquesa at court, frightened by birds
28 At court with Bobadilla, Jester, etc.
29 Marquesa
30 Marquesa
31 Marquesa
32 Marquesa de Moya at court
33 Marquesa
34 Marquesa
35 Marquesa run over in Vespucci chase

36 Marquesa with Jester
37 Marquesa at court for Columbus in chains
38 Marquesa
39 Marquesa
40 Marquesa

Actor track F6 (Beatriz, Crow Woman)
1 Beatriz
2 Beatriz
3 Beatriz
4 Off changing to Crow Woman
5 Off
6 Crow Woman, with crow on her shoulder. Madhouse scene.
7 Crow Woman
8 Crow Woman
9 Crow Woman
10 Crow Woman at Portuguese court
11 Off changing to Beatriz
12 Off
13 Beatriz gets into bed.
14 Beatriz.
15 Beatriz
16 Beatriz
17 Beatriz
18 Beatriz
19 Beatriz
20 Beatriz
Intermission—changes to Crow Woman
21 Crow Woman serving at the Inn
22 Crow Woman observes muster of sailors
23 Off changing to Beatriz
24 Beatriz in bed for Rodrigo accusation
25 Beatriz
26 Beatriz
27 Beatriz
28 Beatriz. The doubt scene.
29 Beatriz waiting
30 Beatriz waiting

31 Beatriz. You killed him.
32 Beatriz grieving DL
33 Beatriz observes Felipa scene
34 Beatriz on ship with Felipa & Juana?
35 Beatriz part of mad Vespucci chase.
36 Beatriz
37 Beatriz
38 Beatriz
39 Beatriz
40 Beatriz one of last to depart.

Actor Track F7 (Rosaura, Crocodile Girl, 2nd Native, Mermaid, Chinese)
1 Rosaura sunning herself & flirting with Diego
2 Rosaura with Diego?
3 Rosaura with Diego?
4 Off changing to Crocodile Girl.
5 Off
6 Crocodile Girl at madhouse with crocodile hand puppet (Maurice)
7 Crocodile Girl
8 Crocodile Girl
9 Crocodile Girl
10 Crocodile Girl at the Portuguese court. Hand puppet laughs.
11 Crocodile Girl
12 Off changing to Rosaura
13 Off
14 Rosaura appears as she is mentioned by Beatriz, the friend.
15 Rosaura chased on by Juana with shears.
16 Rosaura observes royal quarrel with Marquesa, Jester, etc.
17 Rosaura
18 Rosaura
19 Rosaura
20 Rosaura
Intermission—changes to Crocodile Girl
21 Crocodile Girl at the Inn with hand puppet, pig woman, etc.
22 Crocodile Girl at the muster of sailors.
23 Off changing to 2nd Native girl.

24 Off
25 Second Native Girl
26 Second Native Girl
27 Second Native Girl
28 Second Native Girl
29 Second Native Girl
30 Second Native Girl
31 Off changing to 2nd Mermaid
32 Off
33 Off
34 Second Mermaid
35 Off changing to 2nd Chinese Girl
36 Off
37 Off
38 Off
39 Second Chinese Girl
40 Off briefly for quick change back to Rosaura, returns during
   Torquemada judgement

Actor Track F8 (Maria, 1st Native Girl, Mermaid, Chinese Girl)
1 Maria at the seashore.
2 Maria moons after Diego, who is with Rosaura.
3 Maria serves drink to Rodrigo DR.
4 Maria in church.
5 Maria brings soup to Felipa & Columbus.
6 Maria as Virgin in madhouse.
7 Maria with Desdemona.
8 Maria
9 Maria
10 Maria at the Portuguese court.
11 Maria
12 Maria brings Columbus bottle.
13 Maria as serving girl, cozy with Diego.
14 Maria as serving girl at Inn with Diego.
15 Maria a serving girl at court? With Desdemona.
16 Maria with Diego, scolds him for going off with Marquesa?
17 Maria
18 Maria with Diego at seashore.

19 Maria & Desdemona.

20 Maria observes court with Desdemona

Intermission

21 Maria as serving girl at Inn in Palos.

22 Maria observes muster.

23 Off changing to first native

24 Off

25 First Native Girl, meeting sailors

26 First Native Girl

27 First Native Girl

28 First Native Girl (as Beatriz speaks of them)

29 First Native Girl

30 First Native Girl (On ship, cannibal scene.)

31 Off changing into mermaid

32 Off

33 Off

34 First Mermaid

35 Off changing into Chinese Girl

36 Off

37 Off

38 Off

39 First Chinese Girl

40 Off briefly for quick change to Maria, returns during
   Torquemada judgement

Actor Track M1 (Torquemada)

1 Last to enter, UC, at thunder & darkness.

2 Watches from upstage.

3 Watches with Juana and comments.

4 With Juana in church.

5 Pushed about during fight of Moniz and Columbus.

6 Wanders through madhouse with Juana, bothered by inmates.

7 Watches with Juana and disapproves.

8 UR above the bed, looking down at Columbus & Felipa.

9 Watches Vivaldi nightmare

10 At the court of Prince John.

11 Prays with Nurse over Felipa at bed.

12 Accuses Columbus.

13 With Juana at Inn.
14 Watches bedroom scene.
15 Watches as part of the Spanish court.
16 Observes monarchs arguing.
17 Observes
18 Observes
19 Observes
20 Observes
Intermission
21 Torquemada watches from shipwreck and comments.
22 Observes muster.
23 Observes voyage from the dark waters below?
24 Downstage with Columbus for Rodrigo accusation
25 Presides over interrogation by Prosecutor
26 Presides over interrogation
27 At Spanish court
28 Observes Columbus/Beatriz scene from DR throne
29 Plays scene from throne
30 Observes ship scene from downstage, speaks at end
31 Watches upstage
32 Observes from court
33 Observes from U the Columbus/Felipa scene DL
34 Speaks from throne area
35 Gets knocked down and run over in Vespucci chase.
36 Observes
37 Observes
38 Observes
39 Goes to get book
40 Passes final judgement from UC with black book, then
   leaves.

Actor Track M2 (Columbus)
1 First to appear, simple basic Captain's outfit, calm, then
   storm
2 Off, then returns wet in just shirt, post shipwreck
3 Dresses, simple clothes, objective—marry rich in Lisbon
4 Pathetic in church, gets Felipa's attention
5 In bed, just shirt, soup, puts on better clothes

6 At madhouse, has eerie feeling he belongs there
7 Dragged back to Felipa, proposes
8 At the island. At peace, but things in his head.
9 Vivaldi nightmare, dresses better to go to court.
10 Portuguese court. Being laughed at critical to his development.
11 Death of Felipa. Horrible sense of guilt, loss.
12 Ghost scene. Hope rekindled.
13 Sunny Spain. Loneliness of the exile once again.
14 Beatriz. She is just what he needs.
15 The Spanish court. Here he is at his best as a person, with Juana.
16 With Beatriz during court fight.
17 With Beatriz. Too preoccupied to think about consequences.
18 In despair with Beatriz, decides he must leave.
19 Packing for France. From anger to joy.
20 Back at court, slight disorientation of getting what you want.
Intermission
21 With Diego, enters tavern.
22 Muster, lets Pinzon handle this
23 On the ship, very isolated and unreal, anxious
24 Does not want to deal with Rodrigo, has more important things.
25 Really set off balance by Prosecutor. Image of his own guilt?
26 Things begin to go sour. The natives.
27 The birds. This is not quite how he pictured his triumph.
28 Doubts with Beatriz. He tries to reason his doubts away.
29 In a defensive posture. His doubt is the best part of him.
30 Up on ship. Isolated, friendless.
31 Rejected by Beatriz. He means what he says, but then recants.
32 The money scene. He is more and more compromised, losing his soul.
33 Felipa can no longer help him. Lost innocence.
34 The mermaids are images of his own turning wits.

35 Credit goes to the stupid. Undignified consequences of fame.
36 Chains. He plays the role of martyr, punishes himself.
37 He cries. He is desperate.
38 Wants desperately to believe in any triumph, but all is tainted
39 China is not what he imagined. Only a mockery.
40 Authority absolves him, makes him a saint. But he knows otherwise.

Actor Track M3 (Moniz, Bobadilla, Pinzon)
1 Moniz chases Beggar away from Felipa, pulls her from Ancient M.
2 Moniz scolds Felipa in R throne area with Nurse.
3 Moniz as Felipa and Nurse prepare for church.
4 Moniz
5 Moniz storms into bedroom pushing Nurse to get Columbus.
6 Moniz told by Nurse of Felipa's pregnancy, gets Dirty Carlos.
7 Moniz tells Columbus he must marry Felipa.
8 Moniz
9 Moniz
10 Moniz at Felipa's bedside with Nurse.
11 Moniz informs Columbus that Felipa is dead.
12 Off changing to Bobadilla.
13 Off
14 Off
15 Bobadilla at Spanish court, flirts with Marquesa.
16 Bobadilla given message by Ferdinand.
17 Bobadilla delivers message to Diego.
18 Bobadilla at court, plagued by Jester?
19 Bobadilla given message by Queen, delivers to Diego.
20 Bobadilla at court.
Intermission—changes to Pinzon.
21 Pinzon—first to enter UC on music, Ahab line.
22 Pinzon musters the sailors.
23 Pinzon on the first voyage.
24 Pinzon as Rodrigo accuses.

25 Pinzon with Natives, hears of gold, sneaks away.
26 Off changing to Bobadilla.
27 Bobadilla at Spanish court, brings gun to Ferdinand.
28 Bobadilla tries to seduce native girls.
29 Bobadilla beaten off by Juana.
30 Bobadilla goes back to Marquesa?
31 Bobadilla
32 Bobadilla
33 Bobadilla maligning Columbus to Ferdinand.
34 Bobadilla
35 Bobadilla knocked over during Vespucci chase.
36 Bobadilla takes command of Hispaniola, puts Columbus in chains.
37 Bobadilla enjoying himself on Hispaniola
38 Bobadilla scoffs at the warnings of Columbus.
39 Off changing to Moniz.
40 Moniz for final judgement.

Actor Track M4 (Rodrigo, Headless Man, Jester)
1 Rodrigo in crow's nest.
2 Rodrigo at seashore.
3 Rodrigo served drink by Maria?
4 Off changing to Headless Man.
5 Off
6 Headless Man in madhouse.
7 Off changing to Jester.
8 Off
9 Off
10 Jester at Portuguese court. Pie in face.
11 Jester scolded by Juana.
12 Jester pursues Desdemona?
13 Jester drinks with Desdemona?
14 Jester dumped by Desdemona?
15 Jester blows horn, Spanish court.
16 Jester watches argument with Marquesa, Bobadilla.
17 Jester mocks Bobadilla, Harpo to Marquesa's Margaret Dumont.
18 Jester part of Juana/Isabella chase.

19 Jester makes time with Marquesa while Bobadilla is gone?
20 Jester at Spanish court.
Intermission—changes to Rodrigo
21 Rodrigo in tavern.
22 Rodrigo at muster.
23 Rodrigo in crow's nest, spots land.
24 Rodrigo accuses Columbus.
25 Rodrigo accuses Native Girls.
26 Off changing to Jester.
27 Jester at Spanish court. Birds.
28 Jester after Native Girls?
29 Jester
30 Jester
31 Jester
32 Jester
33 Jester
34 Jester
35 Jester part of mad Vespucci chase.
36 Jester blows mock fanfare for Bobadilla.
37 Jester at court.
38 Off changing to Rodrigo
39 Off?
40 Rodrigo for final judgement

Actor Track M5 (Beggar, Dr. Slawkenbergius, Ferdinand)
1 Beggar at the seashore.
2 Beggar gets table for Mama.
3 Beggar lurks to get food.
4 Off changing to Slawkenbergius.
5 Off
6 Dr. Slawkenbergius at the madhouse.
7 Slawkenbergius observes.
8 Slawkenbergius
9 Slawkenbergius unobtrusive so he can pop out in next scene.
10 Slawkenbergius appears from behind throne at Portuguese
   court.
11 Slawkenbergius?
12 Off changing to Ferdinand

13 Off
14 Off
15 Ferdinand at Spanish court.
16 Ferdinand
17 Ferdinand
18 Ferdinand
19 Ferdinand
20 Ferdinand
Intermission—changes to Beggar
21 Beggar at Inn.
22 Beggar at muster.
23 Beggar on ship.
24 Beggar
25 Beggar with native girls
26 Off changing to Ferdinand
27 Ferdinand
28 Ferdinand
29 Ferdinand
30 Ferdinand
31 Ferdinand
32 Ferdinand
33 Ferdinand
34 Ferdinand
35 Ferdinand run over in Vespucci scene.
36 Ferdinand
37 Ferdinand
38 Off changing back to Beggar?
39 Off
40 Beggar for last judgement.

Actor Track M6 (Diego, Two-Headed Man, 2nd Vivaldi, Francisco)
1 Diego flirts with Rosaura at seashore.
2 Diego with Rosaura
3 Diego with Rosaura
4 Off changing to two-headed man.
5 Off
6 Two-Headed Man at Madhouse

7 Off changing to 2nd Vivaldi

8 Off

9 Second Vivaldi

10 Off changing to Diego

11 Off

12 Off

13 Diego meets Columbus in Tavern. Maria.

14 Diego with Maria.

15 Diego with Columbus at Spanish Court. Goes off with Marquesa?

16 Diego back with Maria.

17 Diego gets bad news from Bobadilla.

18 Diego broods at seashore with Maria

19 Diego gets message from Bobadilla again.

20 Diego goes with Columbus to court.

Intermission

21 Diego with Columbus in Inn.

22 Diego at muster.

23 Diego on ship for first voyage.

24 Diego with Native Girls

25 Diego with Native Girls

26 Diego with Native Girls

27 Off changing to Francisco.

28 Off

29 Off

30 Francisco the cook. Cannibal scene on ship.

31 Francisco drinking with Ancient?

32 Francisco

33 Francisco

34 Francisco on ship for Mermaid scene

35 Francisco in mad Vespucci chase

36 Francisco stages insurrection, puts Columbus in chains

37 Francisco brings back Columbus in chains

38 Off changing back to Diego

39 Off

40 Diego for final judgement scene.

Actor Track M7 (Ancient Mariner, 1st Vivaldi, Vespucci, Emperor)

1 Ancient Mariner fishing in dinghy
2 Ancient Mariner
3 Ancient Mariner
4 Ancient Mariner in church
5 Ancient Mariner in church
6 Ancient Mariner at the madhouse
7 Off changing to 1st Vivaldi
8 Off
9 First Vivaldi
10 Off changing back to Ancient Mariner
11 Off
12 Off
13 Ancient Mariner at Spanish inn.
14 A. Mariner still drinking
15 A. Mariner
16 A. Mariner
17 A. Mariner
18 A. Mariner
19 A. Mariner
20 A. Mariner
Intermission
21 Ancient Mariner at Inn
22 Ancient Mariner at muster
23 A. Mariner on ship for first voyage
24 A. Mariner with natives
25 A. Mariner with natives
26 A. Mariner puts on shackles & muzzles
27 A. Mariner leads natives
28 A. Mariner with natives
29 A. Mariner with natives
30 On ship for cannibal scene
31 Drinking in tavern with Francisco
32 Drinking in tavern with Francisco
33 Off changing to Vespucci
34 Off
35 Vespucci

36 Off changing to Emperor of China
37 Off
38 Off
39 Emperor of China
40 After quick change back to Ancient Mariner, returns during
   Torquemada's judgement.

Actor Track M8 (Dirty Carlos, Prince John, Prosecutor)
1 Dirty Carlos with bottle, brooding
2 Dirty Carlos
3 Dirty Carlos is flunky for Moniz
4 Dirty Carlos
5 Dirty Carlos drinking on guard?
6 Dirty Carlos instructed by Moniz to get Columbus
7 Dirty Carlos drags Columbus back to Moniz
8 Off changing to Prince John
9 Off
10 Prince John of Portugal
11 Off changing back to Dirty Carlos, returns end of scene,
   mourns
12 Dirty Carlos
13 Dirty Carlos at the Inn
14 Dirty Carlos
15 Dirty Carlos
16 Dirty Carlos
17 Dirty Carlos
18 Off changing to Prosecutor
19 Off
20 Prosecutor
Intermission—changes back to Dirty Carlos
21 Dirty Carlos at Inn in Palos
22 Dirty Carlos at muster
23 Off changing to Prosecutor
24 Off
25 Prosecutor
26 Prosecutor
27 Prosecutor
28 Prosecutor

29 Prosecutor
30 Prosecutor
31 Prosecutor
32 Prosecutor
33 Prosecutor
34 Prosecutor
35 Prosecutor
36 Prosecutor
37 Prosecutor
38 Prosecutor
39 Prosecutor
40 Prosecutor, last to leave except for Juana.

THE OHIO STATE UNIVERSITY THEATRE
MARINER by DON NIGRO
GROUND PLAN

Photograph by Russell Hastings

Other Publications for Your Interest

CINDERELLA WALTZ
(ALL GROUPS—COMEDY)
By DON NIGRO

4 men, 5 women—1 set

Rosey Snow is trapped in a fairy tale world that is by turns funny and a little frightening, with her stepsisters Goneril and Regan, her demented stepmother, her lecherous father, a bewildered Prince, a fairy godmother who sings salty old sailor songs, a troll and a possibly homicidal village idiot. A play which investigates the archetypal origins of the world's most popular fairy tale and the tension between the more familiar and charming Perrault version and the darker, more ancient and disturbing tale recorded by the brothers Grimm. Grotesque farce and romantic fantasy blend in a fairy tale for adults.

(#5208)

ROBIN HOOD
(LITTLE THEATRE—COMEDY)
By DON NIGRO

14 men, 8 women—(more if desired.) Unit set.

In a land where the rich get richer, the poor are starving, and Prince John wants to cut down Sherwood Forest to put up an arms manufactory, a slaughterhouse and a tennis court for the well to do, this bawdy epic unites elements of wild farce and ancient popular mythologies with an environmentalist assault on the arrogance of wealth and power in the face of poverty and hunger. Amid feeble and insane jesters, a demonic snake oil salesman, a corrupt and lascivious court, a singer of eerie ballads, a gluttonous lusty friar and a world of vivid and grotesque characters out of a Brueghel painting, Maid Marian loses her clothes and her illusions among the poor and Robin tries to avoid murder and elude the Dark Monk of the Wood who is Death and also perhaps something more.

(#20075)

Other Publications for Your Interest

THE CURATE SHAKESPEARE AS YOU LIKE IT
(LITTLE THEATRE—COMEDY)

By DON NIGRO

4 men, 3 women—Bare stage

This extremely unusual and original piece is subtitled: "The record of one company's attempt to perform the play by William Shakespeare". When the very prolific Mr. Nigro was asked by a professional theatre company to adapt *As You Like It* so that it could be performed by a company of seven he, of course, came up with a completely original play about a rag-tag group of players comprised of only seven actors led by a dotty old curate who nonetheless must present Shakespeare's play; and the dramatic interest, as well as the comedy, is in their hilarious attempts to impersonate all of Shakespeare's multitude of characters. The play has had numerous productions nationwide, all of which have come about through word of mouth. We are very pleased to make this "underground comic classic" widely available to theatre groups who like their comedy wide open and theatrical.   (#5742)

SEASCAPE WITH SHARKS AND DANCER
(LITTLE THEATRE—DRAMA)

By DON NIGRO

1 man, 1 woman—Interior

This is a fine new play by an author of great talent and promise. We are very glad to be introducing Mr. Nigro's work to a wide audience with *Seascape With Sharks and Dancer*, which comes directly from a sold-out, critically acclaimed production at the world-famous Oregon Shakespeare Festival. The play is set in a beach bungalow. The young man who lives there has pulled a lost young woman from the ocean. Soon, she finds herself trapped in his life and torn between her need to come to rest somewhere and her certainty that all human relationships turn eventually into nightmares. The struggle between his tolerant and gently ironic approach to life and her strategy of suspicion and attack becomes a kind of war about love and creation which neither can afford to lose. In other words, this is quite an offbeat, wonderful love story. We would like to point out that the play also contains a wealth of excellent *monologue* and *scene material.*   (#21060)
